DEVIL POSTPILE NATIONAL MONUMENT WAS
PROCLAIMED BY PRESIDENT TAFT JULY 6, 1911.
THE POSTPILE ITSELF IS A REMNANT OF A
LAVA FLOW THAT TOOK PLACE ABOUT
915,000 YEARS AGO. THIS EXTENDED
FROM MAMMOTH PASS TO JUST BELOW RAINBOW
FALL. UPON COOLING THE BASALT CRACKED INTO
FOUR, FIVE, AND SIX-SIDED COLUMNS.
DURING THE ICE AGE, WHEN THE MIDDLE FORK
GLACIER ADVANCED FOR THE LAST TIME, IT
READILY QUARRIED THE BASALT AWAY, COLUMN
BY COLUMN, AND ONLY THE MOST RESISTANT
PARTS WERE LEFT STANDING. ONE SIDE OF THE
POSTPILE WAS THUS REMOVED, LEAVING THE
WALL OF COLUMNS 40 TO 60 FEET HIGH.
THE TOP OF THE FORMATION HAS BEEN WORN
SMOOTH BY THE GRINDING OF THE GLACIER,
LEAVING THE SURFACE WITH THE APPEARANCE
OF A MOSAIC OR TILE PAVEMENT.

UNITED STATES DEPARTMENT OF THE INTERIOR
NATIONAL PARK SERVICE

Devils Postpile

by Ron Felzer
with the editors of
WILDERNESS PRESS
Thomas Winnett
editor-in-chief
Drawings by Lucille Winnett

BERKELEY

ACKNOWLEDGMENTS

This guide could never have been written without the counsel and advice of many individuals. The helpful encouragement of several mountain-lovers in particular is greatly acknowledged: Stan Bunce and Dick Rea of the U.S. Forest Service; Genny Schumacher Smith, author of *Mammoth Lakes Sierra;* George Hilton, instructor in geology and geography at Merritt College; Thomas Winnett, editor-in-chief of Wilderness Press; and Lorri, fellow-traveller and fearless typist.

—Ron Felzer
Berkeley, 1971

PHOTO CREDITS

ii	Devils Postpile	Don Denison
vi	Banner Peak	Ron Felzer
x	Ediza Lake, Ritter, Banner	Edwin Rockwell
28	Rainbow Falls	Edwin Rockwell
53	Minaret Lake, Clyde Minaret	Edwin Rockwell
62	Shadow Lake	Ron Felzer

Introduction

The HIGH SIERRA HIKING GUIDES by the editors of Wilderness Press are the first *complete* guides to the famous High Sierra. Each guide covers one 15-minute U.S.G.S. topographic quadrangle, which is an area about 13 miles east-west by 17 miles north-south. The inside front cover shows the location of the quadrangle covered by this guide.

There is a great and increasing demand for literature about America's favorite wilderness, John Muir's "Range of Light." To meet this demand, we have undertaken this guide series. The purpose of each book in the series is threefold: first, to provide a reliable basis for planning a trip; second, to serve as a field guide while you are on the trail; and third, to stimulate you to further field investigation and background reading. In each guide, there are a minimum of 100 described miles of trails, and the descriptions are supplemented with maps, profiles and other logistical and background information. HIGH SIERRA HIKING GUIDES are based on first-hand observation. There is absolutely no substitute for walking the trails, so we walked all the trails.

In planning this series, we chose the 15-minute quadrangle as the unit because — though every way of dividing the Sierra is arbitrary — the quadrangle map is the chosen aid of almost every wilderness traveler. Inside the back cover of this book is a map of the quadrangle, showing described trails and good campsites. With this map, you can always get where you want to go, with a minimum of detours or wasted effort.

One other thing the wilderness traveler will need: a permit from the Forest Service (for Federally designated wilderness areas) or from the National Park Service (for national-park back country). The Park Service permits have been in use for years; the Forest Service permits were instituted in 1971. You may obtain a permit at a Park Service or Forest Service Ranger Station or office by indicating where you are going and when you will be there. The Forest Service requires a permit for a day hike as well as a backpack. The two services will reciprocally honor each other's permits for trips that cross a boundary between the two types of wilderness. The Forest Service permits are also available by mail. If you don't know the address of the nearest Forest Service office or station, write the Regional Forester, 630 Sansome St., San Francisco, Calif. 94111.

Table of Contents

The Country

AS THE FIRST-TIME VISitor to Mammoth Lakes and the Devils Postpile country gazes westward from Minaret Summit, near the eastern edge of the quadrangle, he is stunned with awe at the grand vista before him.

The jagged, knife-edged Minarets, products of volcanic activity nearly 150 million years ago, dominate the skyline. Mt. Ritter and Banner Peak, the highest points in the quadrangle (at 13157 and 12945 feet, respectively) stand to their right. This is great country to climb in.

Fifteen hundred feet below the viewer is the glacially scraped and rounded canyon of the Middle Fork of the San Joaquin River, which rises north of Banner Peak at Thousand Island Lake and flows across the quadrangle from north to south. Way off in the southwest, the impassable canyons of the lower Middle Fork and the lower North Fork merge on their way to slake the thirst of the Central Valley. There's plenty of water here.

More than a dozen year-round streams drain the back country. Over 50 trout lakes in glaciated basins dot the mountainsides. Twenty glaciers and hundreds of snowfields keep them flowing and cold. This is great country for fishing.

Inyo National Forest and Devils Postpile National Monument maintain 15 automobile campgrounds in the quadrangle. There are more than 150 miles of back-country trails with innumerable campsites. Hiking and backpacking possibilities abound.

Behind the viewer is Mammoth Mountain, an ancient volcano. Red cinder cones are just out of sight to the south. To the north and east are explosion craters and an earthquake fissure. Then there is Devils Postpile itself, down near the Middle Fork of the San Joaquin. In this quadrangle the geologist has a field day.

A variety of plant communities — from yellow pine forest to alpine fell-fields to sagebrush scrub — beckon the botanist.

The first-time viewer perusing this vast and varied environment has many possibilities open to him, whether he is a car-camper, sightseer, photographer, fisherman, naturalist, hiker or mountain-climber. He may become one of the many who return again and again. Though the land visible from Minaret Summit may lose some of its novelty, it will remain "not a place to make time, but to spend it."

"Within these plantations of God a decorum and sanctity reign, a perennial festival is dressed, and the guest sees not how he should tire of them in a thousand years. In the woods we return to reason and faith."

Ralph Waldo Emerson

The History

INDIANS DISCOVERED the Sierra long before mountain man Jedediah Smith in 1827 led the first crossing of the range by white men. Several parties under Joseph Walker went through Owens Valley and passed by Mono Lake between 1834 and 1846, but white men had little impact on either the Yokut Indians to the west of *Devils Postpile* quadrangle or the Paiutes in the Great Basin country to the east for several years.

Yokuts and Paiutes had been trading over Mono Pass for hundreds of years before a cavalry detachment — in pursuit of Yosemite Indian Chief Teneiya — first crossed the Sierra in this region in 1852, going down Bloody Canyon, which lies just north of our quad. These soldiers soon returned to the west side, bringing back little more than some observations on gold-bearing quartz veins and obsidian domes east of the Sierra.

Final domination of white man over red was ushered in by the Gold Rush in the Mother Lode to the west and by mining activities in the Comstock Lode to the north. However, in the Mammoth Lakes region, white dominance did not come until the late 1870s. The killing of game and the destruction of natural forage by cattle were among the processes that forever disrupted the lives of the native inhabitants east of the crest. Most of the Paiutes who weren't killed off by white ranchers and miners went to work for them.

Probably the most significant event in the development of man's influence in our quadrangle was the incorporation of the Mammoth Mining Company in 1878. "Bonanzas" that didn't work out nevertheless led to a flurry of mining activity in the Mammoth Lakes area from 1877 to 1880. In 1878 the 54-mile Mammoth Trail, from Fresno Flats to Mammoth City via Reds Meadow and Mammoth Pass, became for stockmen, ranchers and prospectors a direct route across the Sierra to Mammoth Lakes. The droughts of 1863-64, '71 and '77 drove stockmen to the mountains for summer grazing. Sheepherding continued as far east as Summit Meadow until 1963. Mining at Mammoth City was pretty much a bust by 1880, but prospecting and spasms of activity in the late 1890's and again in the 1920's continued to open up the country.

In 1907 President Theodore Roosevelt proclaimed the formation of Inyo National Forest, consisting mostly of acreage in Owens Valley. Today half of the quadrangle lies in Inyo and half in Sierra National Forest. This land is administered by the government largely for recreation and watershed purposes. Devils Postpile National Monument, established July 6, 1911, is the only other large ownership in the quad. So the main economic activities in this area have progressed from spates of mining and grazing to recreation, with some timber management.

These changes have not come about painlessly, and such problems as over-development around Mammoth Lakes and the status of the corridor between the Minarets Wilderness and the John Muir Wilderness — which leaves open the possibility of a road across the quadrangle — will have to be dealt with in the future (see *Backpackers*).

"As sheep advance, flowers, vegetation, grass, soil, plenty, and poetry vanish."   John Muir

The Geology

LANDFORMS RESULTING from vulcanism and glaciation dominate the landscape of *Devils Postpile* quadrangle. Pumice flats, red cinder cones and ancient lava flows attest to the past upheavals of this land. U-shaped canyons, hanging valleys, and scraped and polished rock faces show the grinding force of the most recent Ice Age glaciers.

Expanses of a porous, light-weight volcanic rock called pumice cover much of the eastern portion of the quadrangle. Pumice is a grayish, glassy rock full of holes created by gas bubbles when the rock formed. This material was deposited after the last Ice Age, less than 10,000 years ago, blown from vents which lie on a line from Mammoth Mountain to Mono Lake. These vents were formed when superheated gases and lava blew into the air at weak spots in the earth's crust.

Devils Postpile, from which this quadrangle takes its name, is itself a product of vulcanism. Approximately 915,000 years ago dark, molten lava of a type called basalt poured through Mammoth Pass and flowed down the canyon of the Middle Fork of the San Joaquin River. Here the liquid rock cooled, solidified, contracted, and cracked to form columns with from three to seven sides. Later, glaciers scraped the tops of these vertical columns and left a beautiful, tilelike surface of glacial polish that can still be seen today.

As much as any other geologic process, glaciation has determined what the traveler in *Devils Postpile* quadrangle experiences. During the last approximately three million years, the Sierra experienced at least three glacial periods. These were times when winter snowfall greatly exceeded summer snowmelt, ice fields formed, and rivers of ice began to flow down from the high country. Along the way, these glaciers carved out glacial basins, called cirques, surrounded on three sides by narrow ridges, called aretes, which the ice never overtopped. Glaciers in large canyons, like that of the Middle Fork of the San Joaquin, cut deeper than their tributaries, leaving the tributary valleys "hanging," with waterfalls coming down from them — such as Shadow Creek.

As these rivers of ice advanced, they scraped and gouged vast amounts of material from the underlying rock, and pushed and carried this rock to lower elevations. When the glaciers melted back, they left ridges of piled rock called moraines along the sides of canyons and across them.

Glacial polish, which is especially evident along the Shadow Creek trail and between Reds Meadow and Fish Valley, evinces the grinding force of the ice. Further testimony to the glaciers' power are the *roches moutonees* seen along the North and Middle Forks of the San Joaquin. These are large humps of rock with steep downstream faces, where the glaciers plucked material away, and gently sloping upstream sides, planed by the advancing ice.

The very recent glacial erosion is one important reason that most canyon walls are so devoid of vegetation compared to canyon floors. The ice scoured the sides and deposited the material on the valley floors, where it developed into soil hospitable to plant growth.

Geological events, modified by the effects of climate, determine not only what rocks we walk on during the day, but also to a large degree what plant cover we sleep under at night, and even whether there's wood for a campfire.

The Fauna

EARLIER GUIDES IN THIS SE-ries have concentrated on the mammals and fish of the High Sierra, but since birds are the most conspicuous animals in the high country — excepting, of course, mosquitos — let us here look at a few of the more abundant species of the Class *Aves*.

The most notable bird by far in *Devils Postpile* quadrangle is a member of the crow family: Clark's nutcracker *(Nucifraga columbiana)*. This bird is unmistakable. Usually heard before it is seen, it gives forth with a long, drawn-out, crowlike cry, "khr-a-a-a," as it swoops into the top of a whitebark pine to chip out a meal of pine nuts from the tree's closed cones (see *Flora*). The nutcracker's distinctive markings — gray body, black tail, and black wings with white patches — identify it in flight even at a distance. It is the only large bird so marked in the high country.

Not confined to a vegetarian diet, Clark's nutcracker also acts as a scavenger, consuming dead animals and campsite garbage, and as a predator, occasionally catching insects on the wing. It thus plays several roles in the timberline food web.

Everyone knows the robin *(Turdus migratorius)*, the most common member of the thrush family in North America. This bird is found from the tundra bordering the Arctic Ocean as far south as Guatemala at one time of the year or other. Most robins frequent *Devils Postpile* country during spring, summer and fall, though the author has sighted them high on Mammoth Mountain during a late winter blizzard.

A robin is not as brightly marked as a Clark's nutcracker, but its brick-orange breast — lighter in the female — and its erect stance as it runs about a meadow searching for worms and insects are unmistakable. The clear, caroling songs of males during early season, by which they mark out their nesting territories, are a welcome sound to mountain travelers.

After leaving their nest of mud, grasses and small twigs in the forking branches of a tree, young, spotted-breasted robins group together with adults and work their way to lower elevations, where they feed largely on fruits and berries during the winter. Robins are probably one of the few animals that have become more abundant due to man's changing the face of the earth. Our clearing of deep forests and our cultivating of green lawns serve to increase this bird's habitat. In *Devils Postpile* quad, robins are most often noted in meadows and along streams where there are fruiting elderberry, currant and gooseberry bushes.

Another member of the thrush family, more often seen than heard, is the mountain bluebird *(Sialia currucoides)*. Unlike other bluebirds, the mountain bluebird is really a blue bird: it lacks the orange coloration of its lower elevation cousins.

Its commonest habitats are alpine fell-fields above timberline and meadows of the forest belt below 10000 feet. We watch for mountain bluebirds hovering in the air and pursuing insects on the wing in the open country around Thousand Island Lake and at Marie Lakes, near the John Muir Trail. If the wind is still, we can hear their soft "churr" as they flit lightly about their open mountain habitat.

> "[He] had a pimpled freckled face . . . Peasants claimed such faces belonged to those who steal eggs from swallow's nests . . ." Jerzy Kosinski, *The Painted Bird*

A third member of the thrush family we become familiar with while hiking the wooded paths of *Devils Postpile* quadrangle—this one more often heard than seen—is the hermit thrush *(Hylocichla guttata)*. Adult hermit thrushes have the characteristic spotted breast of the thrush family and a distinctive reddish tail which they slowly but continually cock up and let down. However, our commonest contact with this secretive bird is to hear the male's ethereal, flutelike note echoing through the forest, from early to midseason. His song consists of several distinct phrases, each introduced by a high, vibrant note, and is unlike any other sound in the mountains. Hermit thrushes winter below the deep-snow level on the west slope of the Sierra, but during the summer they can usually be heard along the Muir Trail near Upper Crater Meadow.

The dipper, or water ouzel *(Cinclus mexicanus)*, is probably the most unusual bird the wilderness traveler will see in the Sierra. It is a permanent resident in and around mountain streams from the Aleutian Islands in Alaska all the way down to Panama. It remains all year round, as long as the water keeps flowing.

The dipper is the only bird one will see diving into a mountain stream and walking along the bottom. It is also the only songbird in the Sierra that commonly nests under waterfalls. This is the only avian of the High Sierra that sings year round. The chunky, slate-gray water ouzel was John Muir's favorite bird. *Devils Postpile* country visitors can expect to see water ouzels at Rainbow Falls and on Slide Creek near Hemlock Crossing, and indeed along other permanent streams in the quadrangle.

After Clark's nutcrackers and robins, one is probably more

likely to see an Oregon junco (*Junco oreganus*) than any other bird in the High Sierra—if we don't include campgrounds and thus exclude the raucous Steller's jay.

Juncos are finches, and as such are primarily seed-eating birds, usually seen busily searching for food on the ground under trees and shrubs or out in open meadows. They are small birds with slate-gray heads, pinkish sides and striking white outer tail feathers, which flash in flight.

If one should suddenly be accosted by a loudly chirping Oregon junco — generally an extremely skittish bird — he can bet there is a well-lined, cuplike nest on the ground near-by, which its owner would rather have remain unnoticed.

Oregon juncoes are found from the lowest reaches of the San Joaquin River through all forest types in the quad to alpine fell-fields, where at least some scattered dwarf willows exist for nest cover.

Another finch, and a bird of rather unusual habits, is the gray-crowned rosy finch (*Leucosticte tephrocotis*), denizen of the highest peaks and glaciers of the quadrangle. This bird is unlikely to be confused with any other, for only rarely do any other feathered creatures, much less similar-looking ones, enter their alpine habitat.

Small flocks of these reddish, sparrow-sized birds can be seen through most of the year, feeding on seeds and insects that have blown from lower, more productive ecosystems onto glaciers and snowfields. Only in the severest winter storms do they appear to retreat downslope; they can be found at any time during the summer season high on the snow and talus of the Minarets, Mt. Ritter and Banner Peak, the highest points in the quadrangle.

For many years, a veteran wilderness hiker may not associate a thin "seet seet tseetle tseet" in dense fir forest with any animal in particular. Then one day as he's strolling from 77 Corral toward Sheep Crossing, a flattish, brown-and-white bird about six inches long alights at the base of a large white fir just off the trail and starts spiraling up the trunk. "Seet seet tseetle tseet!" By golly! It's a brown creeper!

The high, wiry song of the brown creeper (*Certhia familiaris*) is not often noticed by Sierra travelers, but it is nearly always in the background when one is in heavy growth of red and white fir and Jeffrey pine in *Devils Postpile* quadrangle.

This small, common, inconspicuous little bird feeds almost exclusively on bark insects, using its tail as a brace in climbing *up* tree trunks. Woodpeckers normally work up tree trunks also, but they are much larger and noisier, and are usually predominantly black and white. Nuthatches are noisier and more colorful tree-stem foragers, but they usually go headfirst *down* a tree, rather than up it.

Thus that squeaking song you've heard all these years, and that brown, mouselike creature flitting from tree trunk to tree trunk, are effect and cause: the brown creeper.

To learn more about the birds found in *Devils Postpile* quadrangle, the interested reader is urged to peruse the bird guides listed in the bibliography.

"Where they [birds] most breed and haunt, I have observed
The air is delicate."

Shakespeare

The Flora

THIS CHAPTER EMPHASIZES that part of the flora we call trees. Not only are trees the most evident members of the plant kingdom in *Devils Postpile* quadrangle, but they exert the greatest influence on environmental conditions that determine what other plants and what animals are to be found. Trees affect the incoming solar energy and the outgoing reflected and reradiated energy, and hence affect the temperature. They modify atmospheric humidity. They modify the wind; they change the very earth itself by their root actions, and by their litter of dead leaves, limbs and trunks which eventually return to the soil.

Lodgepole pine *(Pinus Murrayana)* is far and away the most abundant tree in the quadrangle. It is found from 7000 to 10000 feet in elevation, and from canyon bottoms to wind-swept summits. Lodgepole is easily distinguished from all other conifers in the region by its 2-inch-long needles grouped in bundles of two; its thin, scaly, light-colored bark; and its short, prickly cones, which may remain closed and on the tree for several years. This latter feature ties right in with the ecology of the species.

Lodgepole pine belongs to an amorphous group of plants called "pioneer" species because they are among the first to enter and establish themselves in an area that has been disturbed. Typically, lodgepole cones remain closed until the heat of a forest fire opens them to release the seeds. The winged seeds are easily carried by the wind onto burned areas, landslides, avalanche slopes and road cuts, where they quickly germinate and cover the ground with a dense growth of seedlings.

This pioneering character of lodgepole pine is tied in with the species' intolerance of shade. Seedlings do very poorly under the cover of larger trees — even parent lodgepoles — and regeneration is much better in openings than under the forest canopy. That is one reason why, in meadows throughout our quadrangle, lodgepole pine forest is succeeding grasses. If seedlings can get started in the generally heavy turf of meadows, they grow fast, because of favorable light and moisture conditions. Fires, which kill both small and large lodgepoles, and sheep, which kill just about everything, have tended in the past to keep High Sierra meadows in what ecologists call a "subclimax" condition, consisting of grasses and herbs. These nonwoody plants withstand the onslaught of grazers better than trees because of their shorter life cycles. However, Smoky the Bear and restrictions on grazing in the mountains have led to the invasion of many meadows—Summit Meadow in particular — by lodgepole pine. Eventually the shade-tolerant but fire-intolerant firs may succeed even lodgepole pines in this ecological process. Firs replacing themselves would be the "climax" community here.

Another pine, found generally at somewhat lower elevations and on drier sites than lodgepole, is Jeffrey pine *(Pinus Jeffreyi)*. It was named for its discoverer, John Jeffrey, an early Scotch botanist who, when the Royal Society was slow in sending him his stipend, walked off into the Mojave Desert never to be heard from again. Jeffrey pine is similar to ponderosa, or yellow pine, a species found mostly lower down on the west slope of the Sierra and not at all in *Devils Postpile* quad east of the Sierra crest. Jeffrey is distinguished by its large, stiff cones (to 12″) and the heavily vanilla- or root-beer-scented bark of older specimens. Its 5″ to 10″ needles are nearly always in groups of three, and they often appear from a distance to be clumped at branch ends. Jeffrey may be distinguished from lodgepole pine not only by its needles but also by its bark, which is dark and furrowed on young trees and reddish in large plates on older ones.

The ecology of Jeffreys contrasts with that of lodgepoles in that Jeffreys are more fire-resistant, due to thicker bark, and tend to form uneven-aged stands of trees of varying ages, compared to the more homogeneously aged groves of lodgepole. Its roots were used by early California natives in basketwork.

Jeffrey pine ranges from Oregon to Baja California, and in *Devils Postpile* quadrangle it is normally found between 6000 and 9000 feet. It is common on the trail to Cascade Valley.

Silver pine, or western white pine *(Pinus monticola)*, is one of two 5-needle pines encountered in our quad. The other is whitebark pine. "Five-needle pines" are those whose needles are grouped in bundles ("fascicles") of five. Within this group are also sugar pine, limber pine, bristlecone pine and eastern white pine. Silver pine's flexible-scaled cones are 5 to 10 inches long, and its bark is brownish and blocky.

Once the mainstay of the timber industry in Idaho, this species is being wiped out commercially in the northern part of its range by white-pine blister rust. This disease, which attacks all five-needle pines, was brought into this country in the late 19th century on seedlings from Europe. Like many introduced parasites, blister rust had no natural enemies in the new habitat, and its new hosts had no immunity to it, so it spread fast and destructively. An interesting feature of this fungus' life cycle is that it lives on five-needle pines for part of its life and on members of the genus *Ribes* — gooseberries and currants — for the other part. Both groups of plants have to be present for the parasite to exist. In *Devils Postpile* quadrangle both hosts are commonly found, but blister rust has not yet spread this far south in the Sierra.

Silver pine does not occur in pure stands, but is scattered at elevations from 8500 to 9500 feet, especially in the Mammoth Lakes basin.

The other five-needle pine commonly found in this quad is whitebark pine *(Pinus albicaulis)*. This is *the* timberline species of the Sierra; it clings to windswept, rocky slopes up to 11000 feet. Its whitish, flaky bark and its small, purplish cones — often broken open by Clark's nutcrackers to get the pine nuts — distinguish it from silver pine.

Whitebark pines rarely look like trees according to the definition which says a tree has a "single main stem unbranched for several feet above the ground and a definite crown," etc. Usually they appear as prostrate, ground-hugging shrubs, due to high winds and deep, long-lasting snows. These elements of whitebark pine's environment force the tree into a horizontal growth form — known as *krummholz* — rather than the upright habit it is genetically programmed for. Any branches and buds which in some summers grow above the others on a plant and stick above the snow level are summarily killed the following winter by wind-blown particles of ice and snow. The plants therefore grow away from the wind, often along the ground, and often on the leeward side of a boulder. On barren summits, high winds blow most winter snow away before it melts into the ground. Hence, whitebark pines on high ridges are living under essentially arid conditions, and can be considered quite drought-resistant. Their ability to survive without much water is especially evident along the Deer Lakes trail on Mammoth Crest.

Dead and down whitebark pine wood is excellent for camp-fires, but standing dead trees and branches should be left as they are because their esthetic qualities far outweigh their thermal values.

Fir trees are members of the pine family but are easily distinguished from the pines, and usually from each other. There are two firs in this part of the High Sierra.

California red fir *(Abies magnifica)* has flattened, four-sided needles, which are *not* grouped into fascicles on the branches. Another distinguishing characteristic of the species is its upright, barrel-shaped cones — up to 9″ long by 3″ in diameter — which disintegrate on the tree in the fall and are not found whole on the ground unless they have been cut by squirrels or blown down by high winds. The true firs are the only conifers in the Sierra which have upright cones. Red-fir bark is gray and thin on young trees, but red and thick, with deep furrows, on older specimens.

This species is not resistant to fire, especially when young, and it is absent where frequent ground fires favor the more resistant Jeffrey pine or the pioneering lodgepole pine. However, several decades without fire allow this tree to establish itself in the shade of less shade-tolerant plants, like the pines. Dense growths of young fir trees are a common sight under older pines, under aspens and under older firs.

Red fir is found up to 10000 feet on most trails in *Devils*

Postpile quad, and is especially common on the Iron Creek trail (Backpack trail #3) and on the slopes between Reds Meadow and Mammoth Pass.

White fir *(Abies concolor)* is a lower-elevation relative of red fir. We can easily tell mature white fir from mature red fir by its gray-brown, as opposed to reddish, bark. In addition, white fir's cones are smaller than those of red fir, though they, too, disintegrate on the tree. Young fir trees are a bit more difficult to distinguish from each other. However, red fir inner bark is invariably red, while that of white fir is not. Looking up through the crown of a white fir, we have a much more difficult time distinguishing individual needles and branchlets than we do on red fir, even on tall, old monarchs. Some people tell young white fir from young red fir by looking closely at their needles: longer, and twisted at the base in white fir, and two-ranked rather than coming out all around the twigs as in red fir.

A delicate, wispy alpine species is mountain hemlock *(Tsuga mertensiana)*. Found from about 9000 feet to timberline, it, like its associate whitebark pine, is often contorted into *krummholz* by the windy alpine environment.

The only plant mountain hemlock could possibly be confused with is red fir. However, when the fir's single needles break free of branches, they leave small, circular scars, whereas peglike projections are left when the hemlock's single needles are removed. Both have reddish bark, but that of hemlock is usually flakier. From a distance we see that mountain hemlock has a bent leader (tip) and a much more pendulous, drooping appearance to its branches than red fir, the limbs of which are more or less horizontal. Finally, mountain hemlock has persistent cones 1″ to 3″ long that hang down, whereas red fir cones stick up.

Much of the mountain hemlock in our quad is near tree line and stunted, but stands of good-size trees occur on the Beck Lakes loop above Johnston Meadow and just below Summit Meadow. This is *not* the poison-hemlock Socrates drank.

The broadleaf tree most common in the High Sierra is quaking aspen *(Populus tremuloides),* of the willow family. This tree is deciduous, losing all its leaves every autumn and growing a new crop in spring. Its round-ovate leaves tremble in the slightest breeze, hence the name. In the fall, before the leaves drop, they become a delicate lemon yellow, which turns the gullies and meadows aspens inhabit into ribbons and seas of gold. The sight is particularly pleasing to easterners who miss the fall color of their native hardwood forests after coming west. Aspen bark is white-to-greenish, becoming gray and furrowed with age.

Although aspen ranges from Newfoundland to Alaska and into Mexico, the species is not abundant in the Sierra. We can usually expect to see them along streams and in open, wet meadows, where their moisture requirements are most readily met. Like lodgepole pine, quaking aspen is shade-intolerant and has easily disseminated seeds, so it, too, is a "pioneer" species which invades burns and meadows. Look for it above the North Fork of the San Joaquin on the trail from Devils Postpile to Twin Island Lakes, where it is especially well established.

The Climate

CALIFORNIA'S WEATHer, and hence that of the Sierra Nevada, is governed by what goes on 2000 miles away, out over the Pacific Ocean. There, a permanent system of high pressure called the Pacific High moves north and south with the yearly march of the sun. In summer it is nearly due west of central California; in winter it lies off Baja.

When the Pacific High sits between the California coast and the subpolar low-pressure area in the Bering Sea during summer, it tends to keep the North Pacific's storms, bred in this low, from reaching the state. However, during the winter, the Pacific High is farther south, and also not as strong, while the subpolar low has increased in intensity. That's when storms move off the ocean over the land, and California gets rained on — or snowed on. Actually, it's not all that simple, but this brief sketch does help explain why about 53% of precipitation in *Devils Postpile* occurs in the winter, while only 3% comes during the summer, when most readers of this guide are likely to visit the mountains.

What about that 3%? This takes the form of short, summer-afternoon thunderstorms. When hot air from the Central Valley, or more rarely the Owens Valley, rises up the slopes of the Sierra, it cools at a rate of about 5.5°F per 1000 feet of altitude gain — the adiabatic rate of temperature change. In addition, the air over heat-radiating surfaces in the high country, such as an expanse of whitish granite, may rise convectionally. Individually or together, these two phenomena cause the air to cool and drop its moisture. A thundershower is born. It "never rains in the Sierra in summer," but a poncho or tube tent is not that heavy — and wet sleeping bags aren't much fun.

Summer temperatures in the mountains vary with elevation and *aspect* — compass orientation. Generally, the temperature in stable air decreases by about 3.6° F for every 1000′ gain in elevation. So, disregarding aspect, a difference in temperature of 31°F can be expected between Miller Crossing (4567′), on the San Joaquin in the southwest corner of *Devils Postpile* quad, and the summit of Mt. Ritter (13157′) due to the difference in elevation alone. The average hiker is not likely to make this trip in one day, but the possibilities are dramatic. When we add the chilling effect of wind, a windless, 95° afternoon at Miller Crossing turns into an experience of 10° on Ritter, assuming a 25-mile-per-hour wind there. A windbreaker is another vital piece of summer paraphernalia.

One last comment on climate: solar radiation reaching the earth's surface increases with elevation. There is about twice as much ultraviolet at 14000′ as at sea level, and ultraviolet energy causes sunburn. So visitors to the high country who burn easily, or who haven't got a good tan by the time they start living out in the sun, do well to liberally apply zinc oxide or some other good ultraviolet screen while here.

> "At Christmas I no more desire a rose
> Than wish a snow in May's newfangled mirth;
> But like of each thing that in season grows."
>
> Shakespeare

The Trails

MODERN MAN'S PROCLIVITY to let his amazing muscle and bone structure atrophy while he does everything "the easy way" won't get him far in the Sierra back country. He walks — or more rarely rides stock — or he gets nowhere. This is refreshing for the body as well as the soul. On those steep, dusty switchbacks, and in those cold, wet fords, there is a feeling of accomplishment and of sensuous contact with the mother, earth, which no manufactured vehicle can give. Even calves sore from a long descent, or heels blistered on that extra five miles, are a small price to pay for the good-tired feeling that "Here I am, and I'm pooped, but I did it myself."

But walking need not be exhausting. The attractions of *Devils Postpile* quadrangle are made accessible to a wide variety of hikers by a system of trails we divide into three basic categories: backpack trails, lateral trails and day-hike trails.

BACKPACK TRAILS. Backpack trails vary in length and difficulty from the 3-mile jaunt from Agnew Meadows into Shadow Lake to the 25-mile marathon between Devils Postpile and Twin Island Lakes. There are also numerous weekenders into pristine alpine lakes from easily reached trailheads.

LATERAL TRAILS. Six lateral trails are described in this volume. They connect scenic outposts, not normally visited by main-route travelers, to the backpack trails.

DAY HIKES. A series of day hikes allows the visitor who is not inclined or able to take overnight trips quick access to scenic attractions that no one should miss seeing. Some trails may be walked in less than an hour, but remember, "this is not a place to make time but to spend it."

THE TRAILHEADS

It's a sad comment on our society, but it must be made: Increasingly vicious vandalism to cars left at trailheads in the Sierra compels a few words of caution. Nothing of value should be left in sight in an unattended car, nor even in a locked glove compartment or trunk, especially overnight. Thieves are primarily after cash and credit cards. A car should, of course, be locked, and it should be left in as un-remote a spot as possible for long backpacks. Devils Postpile National Monument is much better in this regard than Agnew Meadows, where several dozen vehicles have been ripped off in one night.

Devils Postpile National Monument: 18 miles west of U.S. 395 through Mammoth Lakes on State 203 (Access to the John Muir Trail)

Reds Meadow: 19 miles west of U.S. 395 through Mammoth Lakes on State 203 (Access to Cascade Valley)

Agnew Meadows: 13½ miles west of U.S. 395 through Mammoth Lakes on State 203 (Access to Ritter Range)

Twin Lakes, Horseshoe Lake, Lake George: 6-8 miles west of U.S. 395 through Mammoth Lakes. Where 203 turns off for Mammoth Mountain and Devils Postpile, continue straight. (Access to Mammoth Lakes basin and Mammoth Crest)

Granite Creek Campground: 30 miles east of the Bass Lake highway on road "434" from the Pines (Access to the North Fork of the San Joaquin River)

Trail Descriptions

(The route descriptions that follow often mention *ducks* and *cairns*. A duck is one or several small rocks placed upon a larger rock in such a way that the placement is obviously not natural. A cairn is a number of small rocks made into a pile.)

DAY HIKE #1

Lake Barrett and T.J. Lake (1 mile loop)

This short trip offers maximum high-country experience for a minimum of effort. It is recommended as a day hike — or even as an overnight backpack — for anyone who wants a beautiful but short hike.

The trail begins at the end of the road that runs through Lake George campground and along the shore of the lake. Our path crosses the outlet of Lake George in a growth of mountain alders and then proceeds along the shore of the lake below some cabins. After about 0.1 mile our signed route climbs upward to the left on loose, shaley rock, past snowberry and pungent sagebrush. We cross a creek which has been flowing on our right and continue ascending rather steeply on granite through mountain hemlock. Keeping to the left, we arrive at Lake Barrett (9210′), which seems to be farther than the ¼ *mile* that the sign at Lake George indicates. Camping is poor right on the lake but better on the bench up to the west. Wood there is somewhat scarce.

The trail goes around the west side of Lake Barrett and climbs a short 50′ to the shores of T.J. Lake. After such a brief walk from the road, one is amazed at the wild beauty of the place. Crystal Crag soars in the west, Mammoth Crest dominates the skyline to the south, and the northwest shore is bounded by steep granite walls. Lodgepole pine, silver pine and mountain hemlock surround the lake, and a small meadow at the upper end is covered by wildflowers in mid season.

To complete the loop, we walk down the east side of the outlet stream on an unmarked trail from T.J. Lake. There are some campsites here, but wood is scarce. Dropping steeply through the forest, we soon see Lake George below and Mammoth Mountain in the distance. Just above a cabin on the lake, our route cuts to the right and becomes a rough, wet fishermen's trail along the shore, through a thicket of willows and alders. When we emerge from the shrubbery, we are back where the trail begins to climb from Lake George.

DAY HIKE #2

Lake George Campground to Crystal Lake (1 mile)

Crystal Lake offers dramatic, high-country scenery and solitude for a minimum expenditure of time and energy.

From the parking area across from the entrance to Lake George Campground, we proceed up the well-defined trail that begins there. This path takes us beside the paved road through the resort cabins above Lake George. The trail may be lost in the tract, but it becomes distinct again just below the top of the ridge directly behind the cabins, where it begins a southward traverse. Here a sign indicates that we are entering a wilderness area where motorized traffic is prohibited. (However, the John Muir Wilderness boundary is actually on Mammoth Crest, more than 1½ miles up the trail.)

After climbing ½ mile in deep pumice, we surmount the ridge and see a panorama extending from Banner Peak and Mt. Ritter in the west to Mammoth Mountain in the north and Gold Mountain and Coldwater Canyon in the east.

From this viewpoint we drop back to the east side of the ridge, and at an unsigned fork our route veers left (SE) where another trail goes right (SW) to Mammoth Crest and Deer Lakes. Our trail climbs over a hump and then drops through mountain hemlock and lodgepole and silver pine toward Crystal Lake, with Crystal Crag dominating the landscape in the middle distance. The lake is set dramatically at the base of Crystal Crag, towering 700′ above. Camping is possible on the east side and near the outlet, though wood is not abundant.

DAY HIKE #3

Twin Lakes to Mammoth Mountain Summit (3½ miles)

For vistas of the entire Mammoth Lakes basin and most of *Devils Postpile* quadrangle, the top of Mammoth Mountain is unexcelled. However, ski-area development on the summit may turn some people off, and the hiker should be aware of nonesthetic roads and buildings at the top. One is well-advised to dress warmly for this trek, because the west winds that roar almost constantly through Mammoth Pass can be devastating even on a warm summer day.)

Our trail leaves Twin Lakes campground at campsite 15W and climbs steeply through scattered lodgepole pine and red fir with some aspen, the latter grotesquely bent by the deep winter snows that make Mammoth Mountain one of California's best ski areas.

Several hundred feet above Twin Lakes the trail begins to level off, and we find reddish porphyry, a fine-grained volcanic rock containing some clearly seen crystals. This rock is a characteristic relic of Mammoth Mountain's days as an active volcano. Approaching the Bottomless Pit — a natural arch formed by erosion through a lava flow — we switchback steeply up through a brushfield of manzanita, chinquapin, tobacco brush, rabbit brush and bitterbrush. Only occasional trees find a foothold in the shallow soil. (Climbing in the Bottomless Pit is a danger because of the steepness and loose rocks not only to the climber, but also to anyone down below at Twin Lakes, so the Forest Service has wisely closed the pit to hikers.) From here we take the route forking to the right and begin a rough, rocky ascent up the south side of the Dragons Back — the long, red eastern flank of Mammoth Mountain — to Seven Lakes Point. When the sun is just right, one can see seven of the Mammoth Lakes from here — Mary, George, Mamie, Horseshoe, T.J. and Twin Lakes — as well as the White Mountains on the Nevada border, Crowley Lake in Long Valley, and Mammoth Crest.

From Seven Lakes Point we climb directly up the Dragons Back toward the summit. The few stands of hemlock, lodgepole and whitebark pine along the path offer dramatic relief from the nearly incessant winds blowing from the west through Mammoth Pass. This pass is the low point (9280′) on the

Sierra crest through which winter storms come and dump several hundred inches of snow each winter in the Mammoth Lakes area. This blanket of snow not only delights skiers but also accounts for the magnificent forest of nearly pure Jeffrey pine found east of Highway 395 between Crowley Lake and Mono Lake — an area that would otherwise consist largely of sagebrush scrub.

As our climb continues, we can see this forest to the northeast, as well as Mono Lake, Mono Craters and the lookout on Bald Mountain. We also get glimpses of the ski lifts and maintenance roads on the east slope of the mountain. A few hundred feet below the summit, the barely perceptible sand-and-pumice trail swings out to the south and switchbacks unnecessarily up the gentle slope. The few wildflowers able to contend with the sandblasting on this slope consist mostly of various buckwheats, and the few whitebark pines that have been able to get a foothold — usually on the leeward side of a rock — are more horizontal than vertical.

From the true summit — a little rise to the northwest across the summit depression — one can look past the structures here to the extremeties of *Devils Postpile* quad and beyond—Mono Lake, Mt. Lyell, the Ritter Range, the North Fork canyon, Mt. Morrison, Crowley Lake, the White Mountains — truly a 360° panorama!

"Woe to those who join house to house, who add field to field, until there is no more room, and you are made to dwell alone in the midst of the land."   Isaiah 5:8

DAY HIKE #4

Reds Meadow to Rainbow Falls (1¼ miles)

Walter A. Starr, Jr., author of the well-known *Starr's Guide to the John Muir Trail*, has called Rainbow Falls "the most beautiful in the Sierra outside of Yosemite." To reach this gem on the San Joaquin Middle Fork, we park at the end of the road running past Reds Meadow resort to the right (W) and walk south down the well-worn trail.

After a short stroll under a cover of lodgepole pine, we cross the John Muir Trail — with Devils Postpile back to the right (NW) — and continue to Boundary Creek (log crossing). Shortly beyond the stream, the Fish Creek trail (Backpack trail #6) continues on ahead, and we take the path to the right (W) for Rainbow Falls. The roar of the water fills our ears as we pass numerous vantage points for viewing and photographing the cascade from the cliffs above the river. Early-season afternoons seem to be the best time to behold the falls and its rainbow in full splendor.

From the most popular viewpoint a steep trail drops to the river, and swimming in the pool below the falls could blow one's mind. Dippers — also called water ouzels — nest on the moss-and-fern-covered walls beside the plunging water, and various aquatic invertebrates line the rocks around the pool. This place is a most delightful experience after several days' camping, and cameras and — on occasion — swimsuits are necessities on this hike.

Left: Rainbow Falls.

DAY HIKE #5

Horseshoe Lake-Reds Meadow loop (12 miles)

This loop trip, which takes us over the Sierra crest twice, is very strenuous and only experienced hikers in good condition should attempt it. Most hikers will probably want to take one or the other branch of the loop down to Reds Meadow, there to be picked up by car or to hitch-hike out.

Past the end of the pavement and before the group campground at Horseshoe Lake, the Mammoth Pass trail takes off uphill through deep pumice under lodgepole pines. There are occasional whitebark pines along the path, and in late summer we watch for Douglas squirrels chewing the cones apart to get the pine nuts.

Our route forks just below McLeod Lake, and we go left (SW) toward the lake. The return portion of this loop will bring us back to this junction from the right (NW). McLeod Lake is the domestic water supply for Mammoth Lakes, and "Pollution is prohibited." (Would that it were so easy elsewhere!) We skirt the north side of the lake through level pumice and then begin an almost imperceptible descent — we have crossed the Sierra Crest. This saddle is not the highest part of the Sierra Nevada in this region — the Ritter Range is loftier — but nonetheless it is the dividing line between the eastern and western watersheds of the range. The runoff west of this summit is part of the Great Valley drainage, which eventually runs into San Francisco Bay. The runoff to the east becomes part of the Owens River, most of which ends up — by unnatural means — in Los Angeles.

The trail begins to drop more steeply and to switchback down, and the forest becomes more mixed, as red fir, mountain hemlock and silver pine are added to the abundant lodgepole.

At the boundary of the John Muir Wilderness, a cutoff goes right (W) to Red Cones. We continue southward toward Upper Crater Meadow, climb briefly, and then drop sharply to a junction with the John Muir Trail in the center of the meadow. Here we turn north onto the Muir Trail (Backpack trail #2) and walk 1 mile to Crater Meadow. Skirting this meadow, we climb on the Muir Trail part way up the more northerly of the two Red Cones, and then we take off to the left (W) on an obscure, unmaintained path that drops across the lower portion of the cone. The trees are blazed, and litter of needles and cones collects where the trail provides a break in the pumice-and-cinder slope.

Beyond the meadow our route parallels Crater Creek. When the trail becomes hard to follow, we cross the stream and find the path continuing down Crater Creek as it begins to cascade over vesiculated ("full of holes") lava. The trail soon begins to descend very steeply, and one is relieved that he's going down to Reds Meadow on it rather than up. After ½ mile of switchbacking down in deep, loose pumice, we begin to level off in an open forest of red fir, silver pine and Jeffrey pine. Large fire scars at the bases of some of the bigger trees attest to fire's part in keeping this stand open and parklike.

The trail swings north and crosses Crater Creek, quieter now, and Boundary Creek in close succession. The route here is level and boggy through red-fir forest. As is common in the whole area around Reds Meadow, there is a profusion of trails, especially in the soft pumice. We keep on what looks like the most heavily used route, leap several small streams not shown on the topo, and cross the rerouted John Muir Trail shortly before arriving at the stables of Reds Meadow Pack Station. Here we can choose to terminate the trip.

To continue the loop back to Horseshoe Lake, we walk north, past the store and resort, to the campground just north of the government pasture. Several old *John Muir Trail* signs along the road attest to the fact that the Muir Trail until recently went through the resort area rather than around it.

Just across the stream, below the public bathhouse in Reds Meadow campground, the second and uphill portion of this loop trip continues. We climb upslope — where trail bikes have been ripping the ground — toward the John Muir Trail and Horseshoe Lake. A combination of high snowfall, springs and sunlight on this west-facing slope is responsible for the great size of the shrubs and trees along this part of the trail. There are bush lupines over 3 feet tall, gooseberry plants with berries more than $\frac{1}{2}$ inch in diameter, and white firs to 5 feet in diameter. In late season it is not unusual to find intact fir cones on the ground along the way. Douglas squirrels cut them off while green, then collect them or chew them apart on the ground for their seeds. Normally, fir cones disintegrate on the tree and are not seen whole on the ground.

At the junction with the John Muir Trail, we go left (E) and keep climbing to the turnoff to Mammoth Pass 1 mile ahead. Then, turning onto the Mammoth Pass trail, we climb steeply through red fir toward the pass. Our route rises at a decreasing rate as we enter the broad expanse of the pass, and red fir begins to give way to lodgepole pine once again. It is heartening to note that abandoned ruts in the easily eroded pumice are firmer than the present trail and are natural collecting areas for forest litter such as needles and cones, which eventually become humus — a component not abundant in these pumice soils. This indicates that overused and disturbed soils can recover after a "rest."

Where we finally come to a sign indicating we are at the pass, Mammoth Mountain rises in the north and Mammoth Crest in the south. A short distance beyond, we pass a weather- and snow-survey station used to gather data for predicting spring and summer runoff, and then we rejoin our earlier path at McLeod Lake for the short downhill to Horseshoe Lake.

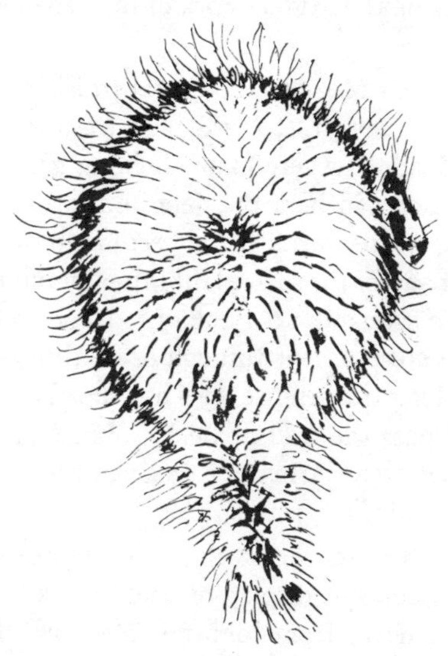

BACKPACK TRAIL #1

John Muir Trail Northbound (20 miles)
(Devils Postpile National Monument to Donohue Pass)

This section of the John Muir Trail takes us along the eastern side of the Ritter Range through some of the most majestic scenery in the Sierra. Camping tends to be quite crowded on this route, and firewood is generally lacking at the more scenic sites, such as Shadow Lake.

We pick up the Muir Trail at a bridge about 0.2 mile south of the Devils Postpile National Monument parking lot and turn right, crossing the Middle Fork of the San Joaquin River on the bridge.

After the Summit Meadow/77 Corral trail (Backpack trail #3) takes off to the left (S), we skirt the western edge of Soda Spring Meadow, where many Belding ground squirrels can be seen. (One can help the deteriorating trail situation here by staying off the meadow and keeping to the left, rather than deepening any of the several ruts already there or making a new one.) We soon enter a stand of lodgepole pine and red fir and begin a steep ascent through deep, dusty pumice. At the top of this long traverse we level off, shortly before Minaret Creek, and pass the trail to Beck Cabin (Backpack trail #5). During high water Minaret Creek can usually be crossed above the ford on logs.

The Muir Trail skirts the north side of Johnston Meadow, which has a magnificent display of wildflowers into mid season. As we turn north from Johnston Meadow, the Minaret

Lake trail (Backpack trail #4) continues west up the canyon of Minaret Creek. Our path resumes climbing in dry, dusty pumice to tiny, meadow-fringed Trinity Lakes, where an obscure fishermen's trail takes off west from our route bound for Castle and Emily lakes.

The Muir Trail continues northward, and after another short ascent we pass around the west side of Gladys — or (on older maps) Vivian — Lake. Here the trail affords views out over the San Joaquin River canyon. To the west, the black igneous rocks of Volcanic Ridge dominate the skyline, and to the east the canyon walls drop away into the San Joaquin and rise on the far side to red-topped San Joaquin Mountain and the distinctive Two Teats.

From this viewpoint we descend to a saddle, and our path leads around the east side of Rosalie Lake (9350′) to good campsites on the north shore, where firewood is ample. From this lake the trail drops through forest via a long series of switchbacks to beautiful Shadow Lake (8800′), truly a gem of the mountains. Camping here is now only fair, due to crowds and a lack of firewood. This is one place along the John Muir Trail that is really being worn out. The soil over tree roots around the lake is being badly compacted — which contributes to root disease and tree death — and firewood is not to be found. Shadow Lake may be a prime candidate for a "rest" — 10 years without campers, so that the land can recover. To conserve the fragile beauty of Shadow Lake, it is recommended that travelers not camp here but stop at Rosalie Lake or continue up Shadow Creek, even though creekside campsites are suffering from heavy camping pressure, too.

After crossing the inlet of Shadow Lake, the Muir Trail

joins the Shadow Creek trail (Backpack trail #7) and ascends westward with it for 1½ miles through Shadow Creek canyon before branching north. This trail suffers heavy use and is likely to be dusty, particularly in late season. However, the dust is behind us where the trail emerges from forest cover and completes the 1100′ climb from the Shadow Creek trail junction to the rocky ridge above Garnet Lake. This ridge is an excellent place from which to appreciate the view of the lake itself, Mt. Ritter and Banner Peak, and Mt. Davis to the west. The traveler will also note the striking change in the countryside. From the heavily timbered slopes of Shadow Creek canyon, we have entered a landscape which, except for scattered stands of stunted hemlock and lodgepole pine, is predominantly glacially polished rock.

From this viewpoint the trail descends 500′ to the outlet of Garnet Lake (9680′). (A lateral leading to the River Trail branches from our route just before the outlet of Garnet Lake. It drops steeply over a very rocky section, in the spray from Garnet Falls, to a crossing of the Middle Fork and a junction with the River Trail, Backpack trail #8.) Fair campsites may be found near the outlet and on the north side of Garnet Lake. There is no wood.

Beyond the outlet of Garnet Lake, one should exercise care in crossing the talus-covered 500′ ridge that separates Garnet and Thousand Island lakes. This section of trail, though well-maintained, is rocky and can be dangerous when wet. En route, the trail circles the east shore of dramatic Ruby Lake, and then drops down past colorful Emerald Lake to the outlet of Thousand Island Lake (9834′). The island-dotted lake's surface reflects the imposing facade of Banner Peak and the more sharply etched Mt. Ritter. Several exposed campsites (subject to a great deal of wind coming down from Glacier Pass) may be found around the outlet and on the north side of the lake. Wood is likely to be found only well away from the trail to the west, where several streamlets run into Thousand Island Lake. Just north of the lake's meadowy outlet, we pass by the terminus of the trails from Agnew Meadows (Backpack trails #8 and #9) and then climb upward away from the lake and onto a ridge along a rerouted section of the Muir Trail (not indicated on the topo map). Along this ridge trail, the hiker will discover a verdant growth of wildflowers including lupine, little elephant's head, sulfur flower, Mariposa lily, goldenrod, fleabane, mountain aster, pussypaws and streptanthus.

The trail levels off for a while through lodgepole and hemlock, and then emerges from tree cover to the meadows and ponds of Island Pass (10200′) where fairy shrimp and mountain frogs — as well as mosquitoes — are abundant from early to mid season. Camping is good here until the water stops flowing in mid season. From Island Pass we drop steadily northwest through forest cover, and after passing the lateral to Davis Lakes, we arrive at Rush Creek Forks (9600′), where camping is good.

Our route passes the Rush Creek trail (described in the High Sierra Hiking Guide to *Mono Craters*) and then ascends steeply through a thinning forest cover to the trail to Marie Lakes, recently constructed. From just south of this junction up to Donohue Pass, the John Muir Trail crosses the southwest corner of *Mono Craters* quadrangle. Leaving forest cover, the trail climbs by rocky switchbacks to Donohue Pass

(11056′) on the crest of the Sierra. This pass, between Dono-hue Peak on the northeast and Mt. Lyell on the southwest, affords great views of the Sierra crest, the Cathedral Range, the Ritter Range and Lyell Canyon. (For the trail from here north, see the High Sierra Hiking Guide to *Tuolumne Mead-ows*.)

BACKPACK TRAIL #2

John Muir Trail Southbound (18 miles)
(Devils Postpile National Monument to Tully Hole)

The John Muir Trail southbound from Devils Postpile tours a fascinating portion of the Mammoth area's volcanic forma-tions and then enters the granitic high country to the south. The route leads from the main parking lot south toward Devils Postpile, past a large meadow on our right through which the Middle Fork of the San Joaquin River meanders. In mid season this meadow is a sea of lavender shooting-stars, showy flowers that inhabit wet meadows throughout the quadrangle. At the south end of the meadow we step onto the famous John Muir Trail.

The well-packed pumice trail passes beneath the pillars of Devils Postpile, and several side trails lead to the top of the buttresses. Beyond the Postpile, the hiker encounters a pro-fusion of tracks in the easily disturbed pumice. One should stay on the most heavily used and blazed route, and watch for signs. The trail is gently rolling here, through a forest of lodgepole pine, red fir and Jeffrey pine, with few vistas to relieve the monotony of the trees. We pass a lateral trail that follows the Middle Fork of the San Joaquin to Rainbow Falls, and then, after crossing a stream densely lined with mountain alder, we come to the cutoff to Reds Meadow. Here the John Muir Trail goes right, rather than crossing through Reds Meadow as the topographic map indicates. The trail has been rerouted around the resort and pack station, so that from Tuolumne Meadows to Mount Whitney it no longer crosses any roads. This change, which is reflected on the Forest Service map *Mammoth-High Sierra,* adds about a mile to the total length of the Muir Trail.

Swinging around Reds Meadow, we cross a score of stock trails, eroded deeply into the pumice, which lead south from the pack station toward Rainbow Falls, the Red Cones and Cascade Valley. This trail situation can be quite confusing, since the signing is indequate. The best course is to push straight ahead to the east and not to go off onto the more deeply entrenched north-south cross routes. Beyond the Rainbow Falls-Fish Creek trail junction, we begin the long ascent out of the Middle Fork canyon. After ½ mile of gentle climbing through red-fir forest, we rejoin the original Muir Trail and turn right onto it. Then, switchbacking steadily upward in pumice, we get occasional glimpses of Mt. Ritter and the Minarets to the west through a heavy growth of fir trees. Mixed in here with red fir is white fir, distinguished by its gray-brown, as opposed to reddish, bark. The ground cover here is rather sparse, due to shade and to the dryness of the pumice soil; happily, the yellow western wallflower is abundant all along the trail in midseason.

After we go by the Mammoth Pass trail junction, our route climbs less steeply, and we begin to see lodgepole and silver pine among the red fir. Leveling off and then dropping through deep pumice, we catch previews of the Red Cones off to the southwest and soon pass a signed trail to the summit of the more northerly of the two. (From the top of this cone there is a fine panorama of Mammoth Mountain, the Ritter Range and the canyon of the Middle Fork.) Our route continues past other trails that lead to Mammoth Pass and Reds Meadow, and descends into Crater Meadow, where there are several good campsites, covered in early season by a dense cloud of mosquitos. In early season the presence of these pests is compensated for by the abundance of flowers — shooting stars, pussypaws and lupine being especially plentiful. Wood is adequate.

From Crater Meadow the Muir Trail climbs southward, crosses a divide, and drops into Upper Crater Meadow. Here Belding ground squirrels keep the soil loose with their burrowing, and lodgepole pine is invading the grasses along the meadow's edge. A long, gentle climb takes us through another long meadow where we can see The Thumb to the north. A profusion of streamlets and springs lines this section of the trail in early season, so there is the possibility of camping here when the more popular sites along the trail are taken. Along this stretch we often hear the raucous calls of Clark's nutcrackers, as well as the eerie tune of the hermit thrush. As we begin to drop down toward Deer Creek on a dry, south-facing slope through sagebrush, Indian paintbrush, chinquapin, manzanita and gooseberry, we get our first views of Fish Valley and the Silver Divide ahead.

Camping is good at Deer Creek. Leaving here, one is wise to carry water for the next three miles, which are dry, hot, dusty, and up. During late season, one might not encounter water again until Duck Creek, five uphill miles ahead. On this long traverse through open lodgepole-pine forest above Fish Valley, the footing grades from pumice to granite-sand, and we have increasingly revealing views up glaciated, U-shaped Cascade Valley and to the Silver Divide. Another pine we begin to encounter as we gain elevation is whitebark pine, *the* subalpine tree of the Sierra. (About halfway between Deer and Duck creeks we leave *Devils Postpile* quadrangle and enter the southeast corner of *Mt. Morrison*.)

Duck Creek is a reliable source of water along this dry section of the Muir Trail, and it offers limited camping even though it's quite rocky and exposed. Switchbacks up the east slope beyond Duck Creek lead us to the trail to Duck Lake, which lies 1 mile upstream. Past the junction, our route swings south, rounds a rocky granite shoulder, and veers eastward to the several good campsites near the outlet of Purple Lake (9860′). Firewood is scarce. The partly timbered, rocky shoreline gives way to meadow at the northeast end of the lake, and cliffs above this meadow give the lake its name: they have a rosy tint during the day but often turn purple and violet around sunset.

In mid season, hikers who seek more solitude than Purple Lake generally affords may want to pound out the 2 additional miles to Lake Virginia. After a steep, switchbacking climb above Purple Lake, the trail levels out across a broad pass. Here, what geologists call a "contact" is evident on the wall south of the pass, with dark metamorphic rock to the east and lighter granite to the west. From the pass we descend through subalpine forest of whitebark pine, interspersed with alpine fell-fields, to the exposed campsites on Lake Virginia (10314'). Wood is scarce around the lake, but the wildflower and bird shows make up for any inconvenience. Before the soggy meadows dry out, they support the blossoming of alpine laurel, red heather, cinquefoil and scrub willow. Birds to listen and watch for include robins, mountain chickadees, gray-crowned rosy finches, Brewer's blackbirds, Clark's nutcrackers and spotted sandpipers, as well as an occasional California gull on the lake itself. Belding ground squirrels in the meadows, and marmots and conies in the talus, are the conspicuous furbearers at this excellent lake.

Where the John Muir Trail crosses the inlet at the north end of the lake, it is underwater in early season, and this place has to be forded. Our route leaves Lake Virginia and soon begins to drop toward Tully Hole, at first gently and then in steep switchbacks down a ridge between two streamlets. The grasslands in Tully Hole are rampant with wildflower color: forget-me-not, buckwheat, wallflower, wild strawberry, pennyroyal and thistle. There is good camping, though mosquitoey in early season, in the northwest corner of the meadow, at the junction (hard to see) with the trail to McGee Pass. (From Tully Hole the Muir Trail continues down Fish Creek as described in the High Sierra Hiking Guide to *Mt. Abbot*.)

BACKPACK TRAIL #3

Devils Postpile to Twin Island Lakes (25 miles)

This trail over the Ritter Range follows a portion of the old Mammoth Trail, which prospectors and stockmen used in the late 19th century to cross the mountains between Clover Meadow and Reds Meadow. It offers the easiest crossing of this backbone of the Sierra from the heavily recreated Middle Fork drainage to the little used North Fork country.

To get on the trail we walk through the meadow south of the parking lot at Devils Postpile National Monument and turn right across the bridge over the Middle Fork of the San Joaquin River. For a few yards we are on the famous John Muir Trail, linking Yosemite and Mt. Whitney. Then we turn southward at the King Creek/Clover Meadow trail junction and begin a climb through lodgepole pine in deep, dusty pumice. Along this ascent we have a nice overview across the San Joaquin to the basaltic buttresses that formed when molten lava cooled to form long, straight-sided columns nearly one million years ago. After the first switchback, Mammoth Mountain and the Red Cones come into sight through scattered red and white fir, mixed with silver pine. Soon after leaving the monument and entering Inyo National Forest, we descend through a forest of scattered fir and Jeffrey pine to King Creek. Take a whiff of the strongly scented bark of a large Jeffrey pine: is it vanilla or root beer?

In early and midseason the observant hiker is likely to see the brilliant red snow plant here. A member of the wintergreen family, it is a flowering plant that lacks chlorophyll and hence cannot carry on photosynthesis. It lives on dead organic matter in the soil.

King Creek offers good camping with an ample wood supply, and yields up small rainbow trout (6-8″) to fishermen. An easy crossing can be made on logs 30 yards downstream below the ford; then the uphill grind to Summit Meadow begins. We soon leave the fairly dense cover of trees and come out onto a dry slope covered with manzanita and huckleberry oak. While stopping for a breather, the hiker has a panoramic vista to the east and south, from Mammoth Mountain to the Silver Divide. Wild strawberries, Indian paintbrush and mountain pride blanket the ground.

We begin climbing steeply into dense mountain hemlock as the Minarets crop up in the north. One-fourth mile below Summit Meadow, the Summit Meadow cutoff to upper King Creek leads off to the right. The topo map erroneously shows this junction at Summit Meadow itself. Summit Meadow (9020′), which was used for summer sheep grazing until the year 1963, has since become almost totally covered with lodgepole pine, a pioneer species which at this elevation in the Sierra is the next step in ecological succession. The trampling and grazing of sheep apparently kept the meadow from turning into forest while grazing continued, but when the Forest Service limited sheepherding to the west side of the North Fork of the San Joaquin, the broken ground here in the meadow was an ideal place for seeds from the surrounding lodgepole-pine forest to germinate and carry on the natural process of succession.

Continuing through Summit Meadow — which is neither a meadow nor at the summit — we enter a dense stand of lodgepole pine and red fir, and then begin a long descent toward the North Fork of the San Joaquin River. After entering Sierra National Forest at the top of Granite Stairway (9200'), we drop steadily on rocky granite footing to the base of Granite Stairway and leave Inyo's pumice behind. Groundsel, golden brodiaea and scarlet penstemon delight the eye as we level off and arrive at Stairway Creek, where there is good camping about 50 yards upstream. Dry, late-season conditions come sooner at these lower elevations, so there are fewer mosquitos here than there are higher up. We continue downhill to Lower Stairway Meadow, which in mid season is covered with nodding lavender shooting stars. Some of the common summer birds seen along the trail at this elevation are brown creepers, white- and red-breasted nuthatches, kinglets and nest-robbing Steller's jays.

After a short climb out of Lower Stairway Meadow, the trail levels off through red fir and lodgepole pine forest, and we get our first glimpses of the Isberg Pass country to the northwest. Soon, however, our route begins a steep, switchbacking descent into Cargyle Meadow, down the northwest slope of a glacial moraine which is a riot of wildflower color in mid season. Numerous small springs dotting the hillside nourish forget-me-not, elderberry, pennyroyal, Indian paintbrush, cranesbill, lupine, monkey flower and scrub willow. Cargyle Meadow, which we circle to the south before crossing the East Fork of Cargyle Creek, is itself a sea of blooms — shooting star, knotweed, wild strawberry and Labrador tea. On the north side of Cargyle Meadow, polished granite bedrock evinces the scraping power of the glaciers that passed here over 10,000 years ago.

Our route crosses the creek, where camping is fair, then climbs over a rise and drops to Corral Meadow, also called 77 Corral (7941'). During the drought of 1877, this was one of the few pastures in the Sierra available to sheepmen — hence the signed designation *77 Corral*. From 77 Corral, where there are several little-used campsites, trails lead to Iron Lake, Granite Creek Campground (Backpack trail #12) and Iron Creek. We proceed northwest toward Iron Creek, 5 miles away. The Iron Creek trail is well-maintained and marked by many unnecessary ducks. It climbs almost imperceptibly through open forest to fair campsites on Cargyle Creek.

Continuing upward more steeply onto a dry, west-facing slope, we begin to encounter scattered sagebrush among the trees. Then we break out into Headquarters Meadow, where sagebrush and buckbrush are being invaded by lodgepole pine and even red fir. This seems unusual, since red fir is not generally observed as a pioneer species in meadow and brushfield succession. Because the vegetation is short, we have a fine vista from here to the south, where the canyons of the North and Middle forks of the San Jcaquin River join below Junction Bluffs.

Our path passes through a stand of red fir and then emerges into Earthquake Meadow, where numerous signs mark a trail junction. A 2-mile lateral leads southwest to Snake Meadow; an unmaintained route to Strobe Lake (not shown on the topo map) heads northeast; and our route continues northwest toward Iron Creek. Leaving Earthquake Meadow, we descend gently through open white-fir forest with a buckbrush and bush-chinquapin understory. We level off for awhile, then begin ascending across a large willow, aspen and sagebrush meadow that slopes away in the west toward the North Fork of the San Joaquin. Here one may ponder the picturesque, snow-bent aspen which are especially beautiful in fall after their leaves have turned golden yellow. They have a fragile beauty that is singularly welcome among the faded browns of autumn.

Beyond this unnamed meadow, our well-blazed trail rolls along for a mile in a varied forest and then drops sharply down to Iron Creek (7700'). Where it levels off there is good camping in a stand of Jeffrey pine, white fir, Sierra juniper and lodgepole. Before the trail leaves this tree cover along Iron Creek and plunges down to the North Fork of the San Joaquin, a very faint fishermen's trail to the river and the gaging station (see Lateral trail #3) crosses to the south side of Iron Creek. We continue on the main trail and descend steeply across a dry, southwest-facing slope covered with a dense growth of huckleberry oak, sagebrush and manzanita. Then we cross a loose talus slide of sharp metamorphic rocks, which could be dangerous, particularly when wetted by rain or snow-melt. After this quick drop, we finally arrive at the North Fork and begin the upriver stretch of our route. We ascend very gently about ½ mile through a series of wet meadows inhabited by willows, tall grass and other water-tolerant species such as red dogwood and aspen, to Dike Creek. Here there is an "Improved" campsite just below a beautiful cascade that feeds a series of pools on the river. Wood is somewhat scarce.

A short, rocky climb from Dike Creek takes us around a shoulder. This shoulder blocks the river from our view, but up and down the valley we can see the typical U-shaped cross section of a glaciated canyon. Then the trail cuts back to the river and crosses over to the west side. (The trail re-crosses to the east side of the river at Hemlock Crossing, about 100 yards upstream. To avoid two difficult crossings during high water, one can scramble along the rocks above the river on the east side, to rejoin the trail farther ahead at Hemlock Crossing.) Crossing the North Fork to the west side, we enter a stand of lodgepole pine and red fir, where a sign tells us that we are now in the Minarets Wilderness. Hopefully, wilderness status will someday be accorded to the area south of here, too, linking the John Muir and Minarets wilderness areas together and frustrating any plans to destroy this pristine country with a trans-Sierra highway.

Going through the campsite here — wood is scarce — we pass by the trail to Clover Ranger Station and Granite Creek Campground (Backpack trail #11), and arrive at Hemlock Crossing (7600'). Here the North Fork breaks through beds of the westward-dipping strata it has been paralleling, and plunges into a wide pool — ideal for swimming late in the season, when the water level is lower and the temperature higher. This is an excellent place to camp, though one has to scrounge a bit for wood. Strangely, there are no hemlocks at Hemlock Crossing, but there are 3 or 4 downstream, where the trail to Iron Creek crosses the river. The ford is rocky and cold. Our route as we leave Hemlock Crossing for Twin Island Lakes is the one shown east of Slide Creek on the topo map. We climb above the stream past penstemon, lupine, azalea and paintbrush. Water ouzels — John Muir's favorite bird — bounce up and down on rocks in the creek.

The trail several times ascends and levels off over a series of benches as we climb up the east wall of the canyon. This steplike relief is largely due to underlying beds of rock, which have differential resistance to erosion. The topography is in turn responsible for the collection of rain and snowmelt water into the ponds we see in various stages of ecological succession — from open water to meadow to forest — for the next 2 miles along the trail. Mosquitoes, as a consequence, are dense all along the route from early to mid season. Stands of lodgepole pine, Jeffrey pine and red fir are interspersed with brushy openings of sagebrush, huckleberry oak and manzanita. Then we pass through dusty "Lonesome Joe Camp" and climb to the easy crossing of Slide Creek.

Here we enter what is shown on the map as Stevenson Meadow, but is actually a series of wet meadows separated by stands of trees. The wildflower show compares with any in the Sierra: shooting star, monkey flower, penstemon, corn lily, delphinium, knotweed, groundsel, forget-me-not and mountain aster are especially evident in mid season. The peak of blooming seems to coincide with the peak of mosquitoes, and insect repellent is essential at this time of year. As the trail leaves Stevenson Meadow and climbs westward above the cascading North Fork, we have better views ahead to the ridge along the southeast boundary of Yosemite National Park, topped by Electra and Rodgers peaks.

Just past the roaring junction with Bench Canyon, the North Fork veers northeast, and there is excellent camping here in a heavy growth of lodgepole, fir and hemlock. From this point on to Twin Island Lakes, the trail becomes increasingly difficult to follow, and only experienced hikers should continue. The Forest Service no longer maintains the trail beyond Stevenson Meadow. The route is often over glacially polished rock, and there are only occasional ducks to mark the path. Where there is vegetation, the trail is poorly blazed and often overgrown with willows and shrubs. However, the rewards in solitude and scenic beauty which lie ahead are well worth the effort.

Our route climbs away from the river before traversing back toward it, at a higher elevation. Then we drop slightly into a meadow, the North Fork flowing rather placidly on our left. For the next 2 miles, the trail alternately leads away from the North Fork across meadows and snowmelt streams and climbs back toward the river on glacially polished basaltic rock. Occasional stands of red fir and lodgepole pine offer sheltered and definitely uncrowded camping. Where there are trees along the trail, the blazes are usually either grown over or nonexistent, so we have to rely on ducks to find the route.

As the trail approaches the stream draining Ritter Lakes and Lake Catherine, it veers eastward away from the North Fork into a long sagebrush and grass meadow. When the falls of this stream finally come into sight, the hiker should avoid the indicated crossing on the topo map, because it crosses the stream where it is split into several channels covered with dense brush, and fording is very difficult here in early and mid season. A better choice is to go either lower, near the river, or higher, near the falls. Once past this obstacle, the experienced hiker should be able to pick out the ducked route to Glacier Pass and to follow it up to the base of the cliffs, where it strikes eastward. The route to Twin Island Lakes leaves cross country from this point, heading almost due west and somewhat upward through the gap that lies just east of the more northerly and larger of the Twin Island Lakes. Camping at the larger lake (9600′) is best either near the inlet on the north end or on a point of the eastern shore opposite the islands. Unfortunately, the only wood in the area is on the island, which is inaccessible most of the year.

Not many travelers get to Twin Island Lakes or to the lakes higher up the North Fork watershed. Solitude reigns. Among the few sounds striking the alpine listener's ear are the raucous calls of the ubiquitous Clark's nutcracker, the squeaking of a cony and the rustling of breezes through stunted whitebark pine. Cinquefoil, penstemon, mountain aster and red heather highlight the glacially eroded landscape with spots of color. The water is clear and cold. And the alpenglow on Mt. Davis and other, unnamed peaks to the north is rarely excelled. The way to Twin Island Lakes is difficult, but the rewards are great.

BACKPACK TRAIL #4

Devils Postpile to Minaret Lake (7 miles)

Minaret Lake affords some of the finest closeups of the stark and jagged Minarets that can be had on a weekend trip. To get there, we take the John Muir Trail northbound (Backpack trail #1) from Devils Postpile National Monument to Johnston Meadow. Then, where the Muir Trail turns north, we continue upstream to the west. Our trail climbs in pumice through a forest of red fir, silver pine, lodgepole pine and mountain hemlock, and then breaks out onto a granite slope, where it switchbacks up beside the cascades of Minaret Creek. As we labor up the switchbacks, we get increasingly better views of the marvelous Minarets.

After leveling out, our path passes an obscure lateral to Minaret Mine (operated 1928-1930). Just north of here is a moderately warm pond with good swimming in late season. From here, half a mile of level walking beside the meandering stream brings us to good campsites beside the creek. The silent early-morning riser is apt to see browsing Inyo mule deer in these meadows. From the campsites, a steep, rocky ascent passes the Deadhorse Lake trail (not on topo map), and we climb through the last timber stands before laboring up some rocky switchbacks to Minaret Lake (9800'). Good campsites dot the northern shore, and firewood is ample.

Settled beside this dramatic lake, one looks with awe on the towering array of arêtes to the south and west. Clockwise, from the south, the prominent Minarets are Riegelhuth, Pridham, Kehrlein, Ken and Clyde. Pridham Minaret has a class 2 route, suitable for the unroped climber (see *Climbers Guide to the High Sierra*). These knife-edge ridges are remnants of ancestral mountains that existed more than one hundred million years before the Sierra was uplifted. Glacial plucking at their bases and frost wedging in their cracks and joints have detemined their striking relief. Minaret Lake is often used as a base camp for "technical" climbing in the Minarets.

Right : Minaret Lake and Minarets.

BACKPACK TRAIL #5

Devils Postpile to Beck Lakes (18 miles)

This loop trip takes us in a long, clockwise circle from Devils Postpile National Monument to King Creek, Fern Lake, Beck Cabin and Beck Lakes, and back again to the Postpile. It tours a little-visited area surprisingly close to the road. The loop may be walked in the other direction, but doing it clockwise avoids 5 uphill miles of deep pumice between the Postpile and Beck Cabin.

The first six miles of this trail, to the cutoff below Summit Meadow, are described in Backpack trail #3. Just before Summit Meadow, we leave the Twin Island Lakes trail and head north for Beck Lakes. After the long haul from King Creek, this trail is a welcome gentle downhill stretch through bogs of willow, elderberry and corn lily, and dense stands of mountain hemlock. After ½ mile we come to the lateral to Fern Lake. This short trail follows the south bank of the outlet stream to good campsites on the lakeshore. Wood is adequate.

Continuing beyond the Fern Lake lateral, we pass several wet meadows and ponds and then descend to the junction of King Creek and the outlet stream of Anona Lake. We cross the several branches of Anona Lake outlet fairly easily, but then the path becomes very difficult to follow where it swings up to the west — higher than the map indicates — before switchbacking across the open metamorphic slope west of cascading King Creek. Watch for blazes on the scattered lodgepoles. We climb steeply above King Creek, with views back toward Mammoth Crest and the Silver Divide, and then drop to a cold ford, which is much easier to negotiate in late season when the water is low. Our route soon intersects the Holcomb Lake trail (Lateral trail #3) at a mosquito-infested meadow, so we hurry on to Beck Cabin, built by an early prospector in this area and now dilapidated.

The Beck Lakes trail takes off to the north at a sign near the cabin and crosses through numerous wet meadows, dotted by sweet-scented Labrador tea and pink-bloomed bog laurel, on its way to Superior Lake (9370'). Several campsites near the lake's inlet and outlet offer fair-to-good camping. Beyond Superior Lake the path is difficult to follow in early season, due to deep snows on this shady, northeast slope. It is best to stay near the stream as the route skirts the south side of a meadow above Superior Lake and ascends through open stands of mountain hemlock and wet, grassy meadows.

Our path crosses the outlet stream of the lower lake just above a grove of mountain hemlock, and from the ford we follow the ducked route to Lower Beck Lake (9780'). Camping is stark but scenic on the north shore of the lower lake and south of the outlet. Wood is scarce. A faint trail along the north side of the lower lake leads to Upper Beck Lake, which is quite barren save for some stunted alpine vegetation. Red algae color lingering snowbanks throughout the summer.

To complete our loop, we backtrack to Beck Cabin and then climb eastward across a slope dotted with silver pine, red fir and prostrate manzanita. The dramatic vista ahead includes the Silver Divide, the Middle Fork Canyon and Snow Canyon, and looking back we have a last glimpse of Iron Mountain and the southern end of the Ritter Range. We cross the crest of the ridge we've been climbing, drop slightly to a wet meadow, and then climb once again through mixed forest. After this short, steep ascent, the trail to the Postpile is generally downhill in ever-deepening, dry, dusty pumice. The hiker now appreciates the direction of this loop.

As is common on pumice slopes, several trails have been cut here by different agents — hikers, pack trains and deer — and it is best to stay left on what looks like the main route, which soon brings us out above Johnston Lake and Johnston Meadow, about 600 feet below. On this relatively cool and shady northeast slope, the tree cover is made up of shade-tolerant red fir and mountain hemlock. On this steep slope the typical tree trunk has a curve near the ground. Snow creeping downslope bent the trees as seedlings. After they grew large enough to resist this force and remain upright during the winter, the deformed bases remained.

After a long, steep descent, our route meets the Muir Trail, which we follow back to Devils Postpile National Monument.

BACKPACK TRAIL #6

Reds Meadow to Cascade Valley (19 miles)

The Fish Creek-Cascade Valley trail is the primary pack-train route out of Reds Meadow, and it tends to be crowded and dusty. However, it leads to good fishing and to a glaciated canyon that to some eyes resembles Little Yosemite Valley.

We walk south from the parking lot at Reds Meadow, as described in Day hike #4, but at the Rainbow Falls turnoff we continue south on the Fish Creek trail, under a canopy of Jeffrey pine and white fir. Compared to most of the trails in the quadrangle, this one passes through areas of relatively low elevation, where we see plants not encountered in the Devils Postpile high country, such as incense-cedar and black oak. The path is nearly level here, but wide and deep through dusty, easily disturbed pumice. Then we come to Crater Creek, and stroll along with refreshing riparian vegetation on our left and dry pine forest on our right.

Our route crosses Crater Creek sooner than the topo map indicates. (The crossing is best made about 10 yards upstream on two logs in a dense growth of alder.) Continuing beyond the Crater Creek crossing, we notice again the great difference in environments between streamside and dry hillside. Along the creek are dense growths of alder, bracken, willow and currant, and such wildflowers as orange Sierra lily, 6-foot-tall cow parsnip and both pink and yellow monkey flowers. Out in the pumice, however, away from the immediate vicinity of the stream, there are scattered Jeffrey pines and red and white firs, with manzanita as the predominant shrub. After the trail crosses an unnamed stream, we come onto a granite slope which in early season is overrun with hundreds of snowmelt rills. This slope is an excellent example of what the ecologist calls "primary succession." A new surface, never covered by plant life previously, is being overlaid with vegetation. Meltwater from winter snows and weathered rock is allowing alder, willow and other pioneer plants to get a shallow foothold on the otherwise bare granite. The trail is blasted out of the granite in places; we have left the pumice behind.

Near the ford of Cold Creek is good camping with ample

wood. From here our route climbs first through aspen and then through a stand of large Jeffrey pine and white fir, with a few California black oaks scattered around. At the end of this climb, we cross a divide and begin dropping, at first gently and then steeply down switchbacks, into Fish Valley. Silver Creek is visible south across the canyon. Lower-elevation black oak and incense-cedar are becoming more frequent as we descend, and mosquitoes are rare on this dry, south-facing slope. Two thirds of the way down, the trail grades into a long, gentle, eastward traverse, which ends at Island Crossing (6400'). There is a heavily used fishermen's camp here, with adequate wood. More secluded accommodations can be found both upstream and downstream, where fallen trees offer dry crossings.

As we head up Fish Valley, open Jeffrey pine stands with sagebrush and lupine underneath alternate with dense stands of white fir and incense-cedar. About 1½ miles upstream, where Fish Creek makes a sharp bend north, there is good camping (after a tricky crossing during high water) on the point between Sharktooth Creek and Fish Creek. Ants can be a nuisance here, and one should sleep well away from any evidence of ant activity. Our path continues beside Sharktooth Creek through cool, green stands of alder, azalea, elderberry, currant and gooseberry. In early season the fragrance of swamp onion wrinkles the nose of the hiker who steps on it as he leaves the trail to skirt numerous flooded spots. We pass several heavily used packer campsites along the stream and then cross Sharktooth Creek to Iva Bell Camp, which is even more heavily used and is not uncommonly littered with dog-food cans and beer cans. (A new, unofficial, blazed

trail takes off up the west side of Sharktooth Creek toward
Lost Keys Lakes; it is not maintained by the Forest Service.)

From Iva Bell Camp we make a short, steep climb over a
chaparral-covered ridge and then descend into the watershed
of Fish Creek again. The stream drops fast here between glacially polished walls of granite, and the trail occasionally
climbs around rock outcrops on its way to Second Crossing
(7800′). In mid season this stretch of trail is a riot of wildflower blooms. Paintbrush, penstemon, forget-me-not, wallflower, gilia and Mariposa lily are all evident. Fording at
Second Crossing is easy only in late season. Above Second
Crossing, Jeffrey pine and juniper alternate with aspen and
lodgepole in the drier, rockier spots, while black cottonwood
and aspen line the stream. At the outlet stream of middle Lost
Keys Lake we leave *Devils Postpile* quad and enter *Mt. Morrison*. After a mile our path crosses the several distributaries
of Duck Creek and then climbs south over a little ridge before
finally dropping to the flats of Cascade Valley.

Cascade Valley is a steep-sided, flat-bottomed valley which
was gouged out by glaciers originating at the Sierra crest over
10,000 years ago. The valley gets its name from the cascades
of tributary streams, such as Purple Creek, Long Canyon and
Minnow Creek, which were left hanging when the glacier
deepened the main valley more than the side canyons. Fish
Creek meanders here in what was once probably the bed of a
glacial lake, formed behind a recessional moraine of the Fish
Creek glacier. As we stroll through the lodgepole pine stands
interspersed with meadows, we see the rare black-backed
three-toed woodpecker, as well as the commoner robin, the
Oregon junco, and the scolding winter wren.

Numerous pack-train trips terminate in Cascade Valley; it is a popular stopping point for travelers passing through, and in summer there is a Forest Service guard near Purple Creek, so one is seldom alone in this place — and that's another way that it resembles Little Yosemite Valley. Where the Minnow Creek trail (not maintained) leaves our path and crosses the meadow to the south before fording Fish Creek, and the steep path to Purple Lake takes off to the north, the Fish Creek trail continues upstream 1½ miles to Third Crossing (in *Mt. Abbot* quad), where camping is good. Beyond this ford of Fish Creek, the trail ascends somewhat more steeply over rocky stretches. Fish Creek, now on the left, changes as the canyon narrows. The water is faster, and the creek is a riotous tumble of waterfalls and potholes. Just below the point where the route joins the John Muir Trail, the canyon wall on the north side of the valley is a sheer, dramatically polished granite surface. Our trail crosses the outlet stream from Helen Lake and meets the John Muir Trail (this description is continued in the High Sierra Hiking Guide to *Mt. Abbot*.)

BACKPACK TRAIL #7

Agnew Meadows to Ediza Lake (6½ miles)

This trail leads to the spectacular Ritter Range, capped by Banner Peak, Mt. Ritter and the Minarets. Some say the alpine beauty of all Sierra lakes culminates at Ediza Lake, where amid towering evidences of glacial and volcanic action, the visitor can readily appreciate the colossal forces that shaped these natural landforms. The alpine meadows at the southeast end of Ediza Lake are often used as base-camp sites by mountain climbers on the way to ascend the Minarets, Mt. Ritter and Banner Peak. Scaling most of these peaks requires technical rock-climbing experience, and hikers who have not had such experience should not attempt them without the guidance of capable climbers.

From the trailhead southeast of Agnew Meadows Campground, the trail crosses a meadow, surmounts a small ridge covered by red fir and lodgepole pine, and descends to the San Joaquin River. This downslope embraces many of the ground-cover changes found in the Mammoth Lakes region. One moment we are in dense pine- and-fir-forest, and the next we are walking on an exposed slope of pumice, manzanita and abundant wildflowers. After passing another route that leads south along the Middle Fork of the San Joaquin to Devils Postpile, the trail re-enters forest cover near the bottom of the canyon. We skirt the northeast side of lily-padded Olaine Lake and approach the river in a stand of quaking aspen. Bridges over the San Joaquin on this trail are often washed out in the winter, so crossing conditions are quite changeable. Usually, one can make a dry crossing during high water by finding fallen logs up- or downstream from the "official" trail crossing.

The trail up the west side of the canyon is rocky but well-maintained. This path rises steeply for 800′ along juniper-dotted switchbacks, and the hiker is rewarded by excellent views of cascading Shadow Creek as it falls from the lip of Shadow Lake basin. Our arrival at lovely Shadow Lake (8800′) is through a granite notch where we have a water-

level view of the lake, with the grand Ritter Range as a back-drop. Fair campsites may be found around the lake, but there is no wood, and we would discourage camping here, to lessen human impact around the lake.

From Shadow Lake the trail ascends near cascading Shadow Creek. For 1½ miles above the inlet to Shadow Lake we are on the John Muir Trail; then it branches off to Thousand Island Lake. Several waterfalls along the creek invite the traveler to stop and rest. There are deep holes for fishing or for swimming (in late season). Then we pass the turn-off to

Nydiver Lakes (Lateral trail #1) and ascend to Ediza Lake (9300'). There are scattered campsites around the lake, where firewood is scarce.

From here one can retrace one's steps to Agnew Meadows via Shadow Creek, but the experienced knapsacker can make an interesting loop or shuttle to Devils Postpile. A poor trail climbs south from the southeast end of Ediza Lake up a steep, willow-covered slope. Parts of the trail are overgrown, and one should take care when crossing the stream coming down from Iceberg Lake.

At the top of the first rise, we see below the glacial cirque that holds Ediza Lake, and to the northwest, through a notch, we have a memorable view of Banner and Ritter. On the east, the massive black heights of Volcanic Ridge dominate the horizon. We ascend through several little alpine meadows covered with lupine, heather and pussypaws, and finally reach Iceberg Lake (9800'). From the outlet, the footpath becomes somewhat unclear as we ascend to the outlet of Cecile Lake. This stretch often has icy snow on it, and inexperienced backpackers *should not attempt it*.

Cecile Lake (10280') has the choicest views of the Minarets, and one will certainly want a camera there. Our route skirts the lake on its east side to the southeast end of the lake, from where we have awesome views of Clyde Minaret, Minaret Lake and Minaret Creek canyon. From here, one can either head back or drop down 500' to Minaret Lake, over the talus slope below this viewpoint. Note that some Class 3 rock-climbing may be involved.

A long return loop may be made from here to Agnew Meadows using a portion of the John Muir Trail northbound, or one may simply be met by car at Devils Postpile, or hitch out from there. The Minaret Lake trail (Backpack trail #4) leads out to Devils Postpile. Those wishing to complete a loop back to Agnew Meadows can take the Minaret Lake trail as far as Johnston Meadow and then head north on the Muir Trail to Shadow Lake. From there the first 3½ miles of the Ediza Lake trail return one to Agnew Meadows.

BACKPACK TRAIL #8

Thousand Island Lake via the River Trail (7½ miles)

The River Trail, which parallels the upper Middle Fork of the San Joaquin River to its source, Thousand Island Lake, is the least scenic route to the lake. However, an interesting and dramatic loop returns from the lake via the High Trail (Backpack trail #9).

Our route leaves the parking lot just before Agnew Meadows Campground and follows the beginning of the Ediza Lake trail (Backpack trail #7) to a fork just beyond Olaine Lake. We take the right (N) fork and climb steeply up from the river for a while, until the trail's ascent becomes gentler under fairly dense lodgepole pine. The sound of the cascading San Joaquin River is a pleasant accompaniment to this dusty climb up the canyon, as the river is seldom more than a few yards away. We cross several streamlets coming down from the Sierra crest on the east before arriving at the Agnew Pass trail. (This lateral climbs steeply through open lodgepole pine and sagebrush to the High Trail, and then goes on to Agnew Pass.)

The River Trail continues up the canyon, passes the Garnet Falls/Garnet Lake lateral, and slants upward away from the river to join the High Trail coming in from the right (E). We climb ahead (N) toward Thousand Island Lake before leveling off in meadows containing several small tarns. Several trails branch off to numerous campsites here, but by keeping near the Middle Fork and heading toward Banner Peak, we come to Thousand Island Lake (9834') and a junction with the John Muir Trail (Backpack trail #1). Camping here is scenic, with magnificent views of the Ritter Range to the west. However, sites are exposed and windy, and there is no wood near the outlet. Better sites with wood may be found north and west of the lake where streamlets cascade down the slopes.

BACKPACK TRAIL #9

Thousand Island Lake via the High Trail (7 miles)

This alternative to taking the River Trail, Backpack trail #8) to Thousand Island Lake affords panoramic views of the Minarets, Mt. Ritter and Banner Peak, as well as glimpses down into the deep, glaciated canyon of the San Joaquin River. The High Trail may be combined with the River Trail to form an exciting loop trip between Agnew Meadows and Thousand Island Lake.

The High Trail begins at the parking lot south of Agnew Meadows Campground. (At the time of this writing, the trail was being rerouted to avoid the confusing proliferation of routes up from Agnew Meadows, and the steep, dusty, rocky ascent in the first mile.) We climb steadily along the east wall of the Middle Fork canyon, and emerge from heavy forest cover to a vista point opposite the U-shaped canyon of Shadow Creek. This is one of the most impressive sights along the route. The gouging power of glaciers during the Ice Ages is attested to by the deeply scarred Middle Fork canyon, and the hanging valley of Shadow Creek — formed by a tributary glacier — dropping steeply to the main valley below. From this point the trail undulates along, trending upward, through a ground cover of mostly sagebrush, bitterbrush, willow and some mountain alder. Each time the trail descends to one of the many tributaries of the San Joaquin River, the traveler will observe a lush growth of wildflowers, including larkspur, lupine, shooting star, columbine, penstemon, monkey flower, scarlet gilia and tiger lily.

Just before the High Trail begins its descent to meadowy Badger Lakes, an unmarked cut-off to Agnew Pass and Clark Lakes (Lateral trail #4) forks to the right (N). We continue toward Badger Lakes, crossing the Agnew Pass trail, which connects Agnew Pass to the right (N) with the River Trail to the left (S) via a steep path. Just beyond Badger Lakes, the trail to Agnew Pass and Clark Lakes rejoins our route. Continuing on the High Trail, we roll gently through open lodgepole pine, and then switchback down to a junction with the River Trail on the slopes above the upper reaches of the Middle Fork. From here we follow the River Trail for 1 mile to Thousand Island Lake, where the camping, wood supply and views are as described in Backpack trail #8.

"You can't get there from here."   Anon.

BACKPACK TRAIL #10

Lake George Campground to Deer Lakes (5.5 miles)

The Deer Lakes trail along Mammoth Crest essentially dead-ends in a glaciated basin, the route down Deer Creek from the lakes being abandoned. This trail offers vistas of much of *Devils Postpile* quadrangle, rivaling those from Mammoth Mountain.

We follow the Crystal Lake trail (Day hike #2) until it branches left (S) at an unmarked but evident fork, then continue climbing in pumice to the right (W). Switchbacks take us up toward Mammoth Crest through lodgepole pine, silver pine and mountain hemlock into a thinning stand of whitebark pine. Where the scattered trees have been flattened into *krummholz* form by wind and snow, granite and pumice footing gives way to reddish cinders.

Just below a fork in the trail we enter the 503,258-acre John Muir Wilderness — California's largest — named for the famed naturalist. This area, first set aside in 1931 (as the High Sierra Primitive Area) by authority of the Secretary of Agriculture, extends from here southward along the Sierra crest to the peaks south of Mt. Whitney. We take the right fork up to the prominent cinder cone in the west; on our return we can come back by the left (S) fork, which crosses a small basin. Much of the area of *Devils Postpile* quadrangle is visible from the summit of this cone. We can make out both the Middle Fork and the North Fork of the San Joaquin, the Ritter Range, Mammoth Mountain, and Mammoth Crest off toward the Silver Divide. Mt. Morrison and Bloody Mountain, in the *Mt. Morrison* quad, are visible in the east.

Proceeding southeast across the west slope of the crest, the trail crosses an arid-looking saddle with scattered whitebark pines separated by large expanses of cindery, granity gravel. Judging by the sparseness of vegetation and the exposure to winds here, one may reasonably conclude that the precipitation available to plants on this ridge is probably no more than that which defines an arid region: 10 inches or less annually. Since high winds accompany most of the winter snowstorms that supply the bulk of this region's moisture, and since winds are most intense on summits like this, only a few inches of snow may accumulate here, compared to the hundreds that build up on both sides of the crest. So this saddle can technically be considered, if not a desert, at least arid.

Fish Valley comes into sight below as our route gets rocky and begins a steep ascent through a stand of whitebark pine. The path tops the ridge at pass 11200′, and we can now see all the way to the White Mountains on the Nevada border to the east. In between lie Coldwater Canyon, Gold Mountain, and Glass Mountain ridge. (Here the trail goes off *Devils Postpile* quad to the east and enters *Mt. Morrison.*) We round a shoulder and drop steeply down through whitebark pine to the outlet of the northernmost of the three Deer Lakes. Wood is scarce, but sheltered sites are on the west and south sides. An inviting little beach beckons at the northwest corner of the lake.

Faint trails lead from this lake through meadows and dense but scrubby whitebark pine to the upper lake (10900′), where camping is most sheltered and wood most abundant around the outlet. The basin these lakes lie in offers opportunities for leisurely wandering over talus slopes, moraines, and wet meadows thick with red and white heather, dwarf willow and Labrador tea. The lowest of the three lakes is the most heavily used, and it lacks wood.

BACKPACK TRAIL #11

Granite Creek Campground to Hemlock Crossing (9 miles)

This trail is one of two in this guide which begin at a trailhead in the *Merced Peak* quadrangle, with road access from the west side of the Sierra. The other is the trail to 77 Corral. This route to Hemlock Crossing begins as the Isberg trail at the northeast corner of Granite Creek Campground. We walk up the heavily traveled Isberg trail along the west bank of the East Fork of Granite Creek. Several signs indicate that this area is closed to motor vehicles.

Forest cover on this section of the trail consists mostly of large Jeffrey and lodgepole pines, with young white and red firs in the understory. When fires are absent, the shade-tolerant firs normally supplant the pines in forest succession. Otherwise, the fire-tolerant pines remain dominant. Wildflowers thriving along the sandy path include purplish lupine, white mariposa lily, and a prostrate member of the purslane family, pussypaws. Old license plates nailed to tree trunks 10-15 feet high marked the way for snow surveyors who came in on skis during the winter to observe snow conditions. In mid season, especially during high winds or in a thunderstorm, pollen released by small male cones on the pines and firs gives everything a greenish cast. Soon the trail comes out onto a brush-covered slope above the East Fork of Granite Creek and traverses through manzanita, huckleberry oak, buckbrush and gooseberry to Granite Creek Niche (8000'), where the East Fork rushes through a narrow gap — the "Niche" — between two granite shoulders. Camping is good here, and adequate firewood can be found upstream.

Leaving the Niche, we parallel the stream and soon arrive at a junction where the Isberg trail continues north to Yosemite National Park (as described in the High Sierra Hiking Guide to *Merced Park*). Our route crosses eastward over the East Fork of Granite Creek, and then passes through a meadow that is being overrun by young lodgepole pine but is still open enough to have a cover of cottony knotweed, yellow meadow monkey flowers, lavender shooting stars and large-leaved corn lilies. We pass the Cora Creek trail (Lateral trail #2) and the Stock Driveway to Soldier Meadow and then begin a long, rolling grind through lodgepole forest. Only the tinkling note of the Oregon junco and the eerie fluting of the hermit thrush interrupt our solitude. There are few hikers on this trail.

At each of several forks we keep left, and when we arrive at Chetwood Creek (8200') we have entered *Devils Postpile* quadrangle. At the next fork, we keep left, following blazes through lodgepole pine and red fir, and finally break out into open aspen and sagebrush. Our route then switchbacks up a dry slope, and we soon come to "Surprise Saddle," which is labeled on the Forest Service map *Mammoth-High Sierra*. Here a fine vista of the western side of the Ritter Range down into the North Fork of the San Joaquin River greets the eye. The classic U-shaped, glaciated canyons of Dike and Iron creeks, the knife-edged ridge of the Minarets, and extensive glacial polish offer a dramatic, first-hand view of the effects of glaciation. Off in the south, the confluence of the three forks of the San Joaquin River is evident, and down in the canyon below we can make out a snow-survey shelter on the North Fork.

Entering a mixed forest of red fir, mountain hemlock and silver pine, dotted with large fields of blue lupine, we begin a long descent to Hemlock Crossing. Our path leaves the topo map briefly here and then re-enters it as we cross a small stream and start to drop in earnest toward the North Fork. The trail soon becomes extremely steep and rocky. Fir and hemlock on this steep slope are permanently warped at their bases, due to the deep winter snows that bent them to the ground as seedlings and saplings. On this sharp drop dcwn into the bottom of the canyon, patches of brush and mosquitoey bogs dense with white-flowered Labrador tea and bracken alternate with stands of trees.

At the end of a 2000′ descent, we intersect the Iron Creek trail (a portion of Backpack trail #3) near Hemlock Crossing (7600′). Camping is scenic here. The North Fork breaks through the bedded rock strata it has been paralleling and plunges into a large, cold pool, good for late-season swimming. Wood is scarce, but views up and down the canyon make up for this slight inconvenience. One can go on from here to the upper North Fork and Twin Island Lakes, or loop back to Granite Creek Campground, using the descriptions for Backpack trails #3 and #12 and Lateral trail #2.

BACKPACK TRAIL #12

Granite Creek Campground to 77 Corral (9 miles)

Three miles of walking may be eliminated from this route if the water in the forks of Granite Creek is low enough to allow fording by motor vehicle. One may then drive east on Forest Service road 4S57 to summit 7527′, overlooking the North Fork of the San Joaquin, and begin the hike there. However, in early season — even later in years of high water — the hiker will probably have to park in the campground and start out from there.

From the campground at Granite Creek — which lies in the *Merced Peak* quad — our route proceeds up Forest Service Road 4S57 through insect- and disease-ridden lodgepole pines to Soldier Meadow. Here two of the Forest Service's multiple-use objectives can be observed. One is grazing. Cattle grazing in forests is not incompatible with other uses if the carrying capacity of the land is not exceeded and the presence of the animals is not detrimental to recreational, watershed, timber and wildlife values. The other objective is watershed. In order to prevent erosion and insure the quality of the water leaving this area, the land behind the sign has been closed to all cross-country motor-vehicle travel. Autos, trucks and bikes must stay on the road, which is designated a "vehicle way" from here to the North Fork overlook. (Timber sales are being planned in this area, however, and conditions here may change greatly in the next few years.)

We continue gently upward through transition forest, made up of white and red fir, lodgepole and Jeffrey pine, and incense-cedar. Pileated woodpeckers — crow-sized, brightly colored birds that drill huge oval holes in insect-ridden trees — are common here. Just before the end of the roadway, a sign says we are on the Mammoth Trail System. One of the oldest trails across the Sierra, it was used chiefly by stockmen, sheepherders and prospectors going to Old Mammoth and the meadows in between. In fact, sheep were taken across the North Fork for summer grazing until 1963.

Before beginning our long 1500′ descent to Sheep Crossing, we have excellent views in the east of the Ritter Range and the North Fork canyon. The trail through typical mid-Sierra transition forest is largely granite and quite rocky. The forest here includes Jeffrey pine, sugar pine, white fir, incense-cedar, and also the deciduous California black oak. This vegetation is rather unusual for *Devils Postpile* quadrangle, which is generally covered by forests of lodgepole pine, a higher-elevation species than those encountered on this slope.

Numerous streamlets and springs occur along the trail and give moisture to a variety of herbs, including orange Sierra lily, red-and-yellow columbine, pink cranesbill, yellow groundsel and lavender shooting star. Occasional azaleas covered with fragrant white blooms perfume the air as we descend through this delightfully varied forest. Near the bottom of the canyon, large flocks of bandtailed pigeons can be seen in the California black oaks, one of their favored foods being the acorns of the trees.

At Sheep Crossing (6000′) the trail crosses a suspension bridge over the North Fork of the San Joaquin and immediately begins a series of long switchbacks up the dry, west-facing wall of the canyon. The contrast between the environment and vegetation on this side and those on the slope we just came down is an ecological lesson. Here the hot afternoon sun's rays strike the ground nearly perpendicularly. We see much more open ground, brushfields of manzanita and huckleberry oak, and a predominance of black oak and Jeffrey pine — all characteristic of drier sites at this elevation.

The ascent up this side of the canyon is much shorter than the previous descent, and it is not too long before we are climbing only moderately into a cooler forest of red and white fir, incense-cedar, black oak and Jeffrey pine. At the upper end of Snake Meadow a trail heads north to Earthquake Meadow, where it meets the Iron Creek trail (part of Backpack trail #3) going to Iron Creek and Hemlock Crossing. We continue eastward and upward toward 77 Corral, through cathedral-like stands of white fir and Jeffrey pine. Mule deer, abundant

Red fox

here, are most likely to be seen early or late in the day, when they feed most actively. The West Fork of Cargyle Creek is a favored watering place, particularly in autumn, when water is scarce elsewhere. Scattered clumps of bitter cherry delight the eye and the nose in early season, when these short trees are in blossom, and they please the eye again in fall, when their delicately yellow-tinted leaves tremble in the breeze.

Our path crosses an opening richly endowed in mid season with creamy Mariposa lilies, purple delphiniums and yellow monkey flowers, and then arrives at 77 Corral (7941'). 77 Corral was named for 1877, a year of widespread drought when this was one of the few green spots in the mountains. Labeled *Corral Meadow* on the topo map, it is little used today. Several campsites are located around the meadow. Firewood is abundant, but water may be a problem in late season. However, routes to Twin Island Lakes and Devils Postpile (Backpack trail #3) and to Iron Lake pass through or start at 77 Corral, so most hikers probably will use this only as a rest stop on their way east or west across the mountains.

LATERAL TRAIL #1

Shadow Creek Trail to Nydiver Lakes (1 mile)

Nydiver Lakes offer an alternative to the overcrowded camping conditions normally encountered along the Shadow Creek trail from Shadow Lake to Ediza Lake. They also offer base camps for ascending Mt. Ritter and Banner Peak.

The trail to Nydiver Lakes is not shown on the topo map, nor is it maintained by the Forest Service; however, it is signed — on the Shadow Creek trail about 1 mile below Ediza Lake. Heading north, we switchback steeply up through mountain hemlock, lodgepole pine, manzanita and sagebrush, and then cross the Nydiver Lakes outlet stream — dry in late season — several times, before arriving at the unnamed pond north of the lowest of the three lakes. There is evidence of mining exploration throughout the area, especially near this pond, a practice allowed under provisions of the Wilderness Act of 1964. However, active mining here ceased with the closing down of the old Minaret Mine in 1930. The exploratory cuts seen here are remnants of Climax Molybdenum Company's extensive 1956 explorations. The ore proved to be noncommercial.

We skirt the south side of this pond and climb over a low saddle above the lowest of the Nydiver Lakes. Only a few whitebark pines, mountain hemlocks and lodgepole pines can live in this glaciated trough, so firewood is hard to come by. Good sites with close-up views of Mt. Ritter and Banner Peak are near the inlet.

A route up the left (S) side of the inlet leads to middle Nydiver Lake. Here there are no trees, and the few flat spots for camping lie north of the lake and near the outlet. Mountain bluebirds — nearly all blue, unlike their lowland cousins with orange markings — flit from boulder to boulder in pursuit of their insect prey. We walk around the south side of the middle lake and climb to the highest one, where camping spots are exposed and there is no wood. Here we have fantastic closeups of Banner Peak, Mt. Ritter and the Minarets, and we can even see across Owens Valley to the White Mountains.

LATERAL TRAIL #2

The Niche to the North Fork Gaging Station (7 miles)

This lateral leads to good fishing and secluded camping on the San Joaquin North Fork. It leaves the Granite Creek Campground-Hemlock Crossing trail (Backpack trail #11) about ½ mile north of the Niche, which lies just off the *Devils Postpile* quadrangle in *Merced Peak*.

Our dusty path first passes through a stand of red fir and lodgepole pine, and then, after crossing the Stock Driveway from Soldier Meadow, it begins dropping along the south side of Cora Creek (dry in late season). As the descent becomes steeper, the North Fork Canyon and the west side of the Ritter Range near Iron Mountain come into sight. One cannot help noticing the contrast in vegetation between the cool, moist, north-facing slope we are walking down and the dry, south-facing slope across Cora Creek. Whereas this shadier side has a dense cover of white fir, willow and dwarf maple, the opposing side is mostly covered with brush, huckleberry oak and manzanita.

We continue to drop over several steplike benches down to the North Fork of the San Joaquin, where there is a campsite with a table and fireplace. A small car on a cable that crosses the river here has been used by snow surveyors in winter. Fording is easy here only in late season, when snowmelt run-off is at a minimum; one must be cautious crossing the stream earlier in the year. Our route continues up the east side of the North Fork, where conditions are somewhat drier and the dominant plants are drought-resistant huckleberry oak, manzanita and juniper, with occasional Jeffrey pines. The trail leaves the river and makes a short, steep ascent, up what becomes a cascading streamlet in early season, to the bench where Lily Lake lies behind a *roche moutonee* (see *Geology*) above the river. This lake is undergoing succession from pond to forest, as litter and silt over the centuries have been filling it in and terrestrial plants have encroached from the surrounding forest. In late season red-brown bracken, golden aspens and yellow willows give Lily Lake a welcome tint of fall color. We climb slightly beyond Lily Lake and then descend to a good, well-developed campsite on a bench just above the river. Wood here is adequate. One quarter mile beyond this campsite is a snow-survey shelter used by snow surveyors who come in on skis to measure the depth and density of winter snows. These data are used to predict spring and summer run-off in the San Joaquin Valley. However, most of this work is now being done by air reconnaissance and Southern California Edison plans to dismantle and remove the cabin.

A ducked trail ends ¼ mile beyond the shelter at another cable-car crossing, this one to the gaging station on the west side of the river. Beyond the gaging station a faint, rough fishermen's trail continues upstream to the mouth of Iron Creek. A difficult, mostly cross-country route may be followed by the experienced hiker up the right side of the Iron Creek cataracts. Above the cataracts a fording of Iron Creek may be made to the Iron Creek trail (Backpack trail #3), where camping is good.

LATERAL TRAIL #3

Beck Lakes Loop to Holcomb Lake and Ashley Lake
(1½ miles to each)

This trail offers limited but secluded camping at the base of Iron Mountain and the southern extension of the Ritter Range.

The Holcomb Lake trail takes off across King Creek from the Beck Lakes loop about ¼ mile south of Beck Cabin. Early in the season, the meadow at this junction is one of the best in the quadrangle for mosquitoes and therefore one of the worst for people; camping is poor at this time of the year. Wood is scarce.

We stay on the most-used trail, across exposed metamorphic rocks dotted with mountain hemlock and lodgepole pine. Ahead, Iron Mountain looms upward. After ½ mile of easy walking we come to the signed junction of the routes to Holcomb Lake and Ashley Lake. Like so many wooden signs and signposts in this area, the sign here was broken off and lying on the ground due, to heavy winter snows, when we scouted this trail. The Forest Service should be notified of these damaged signs so they can be repaired, or even replaced by signs bolted to rocks — a plan now being considered.

Our route to Holcomb Lake goes right, and we head up a gully with low walls of metamorphic rock on both sides. The path soon emerges from this gully and drops around the northeast corner of small, warm Noname Lake. Wood is adequate for camping. Beyond this lake we pass a small pond and then arrive at Holcomb Lake (9500′). Fair campsites are scattered around the lake, and wood is scarce. During early and mid season, however, willow thickets around the lake offer nesting and feeding cover and song perches for the natty, distinctively marked white-crowned sparrow, a summer resident in much of the High Sierra that adds much to one's wilderness experience.

Back at the trail junction, Ashley Lake lies to the left. We cross the Holcomb Lake outlet stream, and the trail soon disappears, near a big bend in the creek from Ashley Lake. However, a short cross-country ramble up either side of the Ashley Lake outlet under mountain hemlock and whitebark pine brings one to the lake. Campsites are scarce, and there is little wood; but Iron Mountain and its glacier looming above make this a much more scenic spot than Holcomb Lake. Iron Mountain is easily climbed from Ashley Lake (see *A Climber's Guide to the High Sierra*).

LATERAL TRAIL #4

High Trail to Agnew Pass, Clark Lakes and Badger Lakes (2 miles)

This lateral from the High Trail (Backpack trail #9) takes us over the Sierra crest at Agnew Pass into the drainage of Rush Creek at Clark Lakes. (For trail connections beyond Clark Lakes, see the High Sierra Hiking Guide to *Mono Craters*.) After swinging by most of the Clark Lakes, this lateral returns to the High Trail just west of Badger Lakes.

About one mile southeast of Badger Lakes, the High Trail from Agnew Meadows begins a gentle descent. Here our unmarked lateral to Agnew Pass and Clark Lakes forks to the right (N). We take it and traverse a slope covered with sagebrush and scattered lodgepole pine. Purplish mountain aster, scarlet gilia and yellowish mule ears are seen from mid to late season. Before arriving at Agnew Pass, we pass an unmarked trail to the right (E) which goes toward the saddle between Carson Peak and San Joaquin Mountain. However, it is no longer maintained and is very difficult to follow. Beyond this junction our route soon intersects the Agnew Pass trail and we turn right (N) onto it. A few yards up this trail we cross Agnew Pass at Summit Lake, where camping is good from early to mid season. Later, the water becomes stagnant.

About ¼ mile beyond Agnew Pass our trail circles the largest of the Clark Lakes, and we pass the trail to Lower Rush Meadow and Gem Lake (described in the High Sierra Hiking Guide to *Mono Craters*) at its outlet. Camping is good east and west of the lake, though firewood is scarce.

The trail continues around the west side of this lake and climbs through open whitebark pine and mountain hemlock past several other lakes of the Clark Lakes group, which may be dry in late season after a mild winter. Beyond the last of the Clark Lakes, we glimpse Thousand Island Lake and Banner Peak before dropping through open lodgepole, sagebrush and snowberry toward Badger Lakes, visible below. Our route rejoins the High Trail about ¼ mile west of Badger Lakes, at a point which at this writing was marked only by a broken sign lying on the ground.

Backpackers

THERE ARE AS MANY REA-sons for backpacking as there are backpackers. One of the most frequently cited reasons has something to do with "getting away from it all," and this usually means going where there aren't many other people.

It has been claimed that the density of humanity in the mountains varies inversely with the *square of the distance* from a road, and with the *cube of the elevation* above the road. To this might be added a third exponent: the density of humanity also varies inversely with the *fourth power of a route's "off-trail-ness,"* meaning the degree to which it is poorly marked or cross country. The hiker planning a trip in *Devils Postpile* can, by combining the trail descriptions and mileages with the trail profiles in this volume, obtain a pretty fair idea of the probability of finding seclusion here.

The great increase in the use of the mountains for recreational pursuits has raised the question of just how many of us the land can handle. Overuse in *Devils Postpile* quad is evident in many places: the deeply eroded, multi-track pumice trails, especially near the Postpile; the nearly total lack of wood at the most popular campsites along the Muir Trail, such as Thousand Island Lake, Garnet Lake, Shadow Lake and Purple Lake; and accumulations of garbage and cans along Fish Creek. At various places in this guide, we recommend ways the individual hiker can lessen his impact on the most heavily used areas — usually by camping someplace else and using a stove instead of wood fires. However, some students and administrators of recreation areas foresee — in the not-too-distant future — a need to close popular sites for a decade or more, so they can recover (as has been done, for example, on some islands of the Boundary Waters Canoe Area in Minnesota), or even to set up a system of reservations for using wilderness areas. These procedures would allow, among other things, compacted soil over suffocating tree roots to regain its porosity, and human wastes to decay and be recycled.

The help of wilderness advocates in implementing the provisions of the federal Wilderness Act by 1974 is vital also. Federal lands of wilderness quality in National Parks, Forests and Wildlife Refuges must be proposed to Congress for reservation in the time period 1964-1974. Several groups outside the federal agencies involved, such as the Wilderness Society, the Sierra Club and Friends of the Earth, are engaged in reviewing lands for possible inclusion in our national wilderness preservation system. Whatever is not set aside before 1974 probably never will be set aside. And the more land reserved, the less — hopefully — will be the impact on any one spot. Active participation in the wilderness classification programs of the aforementioned organizations by concerned readers of this guide is welcome. Field surveys and write-ups of areas for the consideration of Congress are being done now. If seclusion and wildness are to "preserve the world," in the words of Thoreau, they must be retained today.

> "When you speculate at random, you solve problems you didn't know you had."   A. Seibel

Climbers

CLIMBERS, BECAUSE THEY GO up, and off the trails, are generally pretty much by themselves in *Devils Postpile* quadrangle. Most of the spectacular and challenging mountaineering of the quad is concentrated in the Ritter Range, between Mt. Davis on the north and Iron Mountain on the south. There are a number of easy summits along the crest of the Sierra, and one, Mammoth Mountain, is described in this guide as a day hike.

The climbing difficulty of a peak is rated on a scale of 1 through 6.

The peaks listed below have class 1 or 2 routes which in most years can be ascended without ropes or technical rock-climbing equipment. See *Climber's Guide to the High Sierra,* published by the Sierra Club, for more details on approaches and routes. Individual Minarets are mapped in the *Climbers Guide.*

Mt. Davis	Red Cones
Banner Pk.	Crystal Crag
Mt. Ritter (difficult 2)	Mammoth Mountain
Starr Minaret	Carson Pk.
Pridham Minaret	San Joaquin Mountain
Iron Mountain	Two Teats

"A common stratagem of those who wish to escape the swirling currents of change is to stand on high moral ground."
                                                                                John Gardner

BIBLIOGRAPHY

Books

Farquhar, Francis P., *History of the Sierra Nevada,* U.C. Press, Berkeley, 1969.

McMinn, Howard E. and Evelyn Maino, *Pacific Coast Trees,* U.C. Press, Berkeley, 1959.

Manning, Harvey, ed., *Mountaineering, the Freedom of the Hills,* The Mountaineers, Seattle, 1967.

Munz, Philip A., *California Mountain Wildflowers,* U.C. Press, Berkeley, 1969.

Peterson, Roger Tory, *A Field Guide to Western Birds,* Houghton, Boston, 1968.

Robbins, Chandler, S., *et al., Birds of North America,* Golden, New York, 1966.

Starr, Walter A. Jr., *Starr's Guide to the John Muir Trail,* Sierra Club, San Francisco, 1970.

Storer, Tracy I. and Robert L. Usinger, *Sierra Nevada Natural History,* U.C. Press, Berkeley, 1963.

Voge, Hervey, *Climber's Guide to the High Sierra,* Sierra Club, San Francisco, 1965.

Pamphlets

Huber, N. K., and Rinehart, C. D., *Cenozoic Volcanic Rocks of the Devils Postpile Quadrangle, Eastern Sierra Nevada, California,* U.S. Geological Survey, 1967.

U.S. Department of Agriculture, Forest Service, *Search for Solitude,* Washington, 1970.

Articles

Cooper, Charles F., "The Ecology of Fire," *Scientific American Offprints,* #1099, April 1961.

Oberle, Mark, "Forest Fires: Suppression Policy Has Its Ecological Drawbacks," *Science* vol. 165, pp. 568-571, 8 August 1969.

Weaver, Harold, and Biswell, Harold, "How Fire Helps the Big Trees," *National Parks Magazine,* July 1969.

Other Wilderness Press Publications

Schumacher, Genny, *The Mammoth Lakes Sierra* (1969).

Schwenke, Karl, and Winnett, Thomas, *Sierra North* (revised 1971).

Winnett, Thomas (ed.), *High Sierra Hiking Guide to Tuolumne Meadows* (1970).

Index